WINE AND BREAD

WINE AND BREAD

BY PHOTINA RECH, OSB

TRANSLATED BY HEINZ R. KUEHN

WIPF & STOCK · Eugene, Oregon

Wipf and Stock Publishers
199 W 8th Ave, Suite 3
Eugene, OR 97401

Wine and Bread
By Rech, Photina, OSB and Kuehn, Heinz R.

ISBN 13: 978-1-61097-774-6
Publication date 8/15/2011
Previously published by Liturgy Training Publications, 1998

This volume is an excerpt from Inbild des Kosmos by Photina Rech, OSB.
Used with permission of Benediktinerinnenabtei vom Hl. Kreuz Herstelle.

INTRODUCTION

This book was excerpted from a 1966 German book entitled *Inbild des Kosmos: Eine Symbolik der Schöpfung,* or, in English, "Key to the Cosmos: A Symbolism of Creation." It was written by a Benedictine nun, Photina Rech. Since she is unknown in the United States, a sketch of her life may be useful not only as an introduction to the author but also as an explanation of her voluminous work and of our reasons for making these chapters from her book available in English translation.

Amalie Katharina Rech was born in 1914 in a village in Saarland, which is now part of the Federal Republic of Germany. She was the second of five children of a teacher, August Rech, and his wife Katharina. After August returned from his service in the First World War, the family moved to another village near the capital of Saarland.

Reared by parents who were deeply committed to their Catholic faith, Amalie had a happy childhood. In 1924 she was enrolled in a girls' preparatory school in Saarbrücken run by Ursuline nuns. An outstanding student from the beginning, she graduated in 1933 with highest honors. A priest who was a close friend of the family recognized Amalie's strong religious disposition and took her into his care to give her faith a firm foundation in Catholic doctrine and practice. Gradually, amidst doubts and scruples, she began to realize that she might have a vocation to religious life in a convent. After spending two weeks at the Benedictine Archabbey of Saint Martin in Beuron, she was certain that she would seek to join a religious order whose life was formed by the cultivation of the liturgy. Her parents were at first opposed to her decision but eventually relented.

In 1934 she visited the Benedictine Abbey of the Holy Cross in Herstelle, a small town in Westphalia. This abbey was founded in 1657 by the Minorites, a branch of the Franciscan order, and had been taken over by Benedictine nuns in 1899. The Abbey of the Holy Cross maintained close connections with the abbey in Beuron and with the Abbey of Maria Laach in the Rhineland, a pioneering center of the liturgical movement.

In 1935 Amalie was accepted as a Benedictine novice. She took the name "Photina," Greek for "luminous," a name that tradition ascribes to the Samaritan woman at the well in the Gospel of John (4:5–42). In 1939 Sister Photina took her final vows. "I encountered a life of such abundance as I would never have expected," she told her community. "I was in my element and felt happy from the very first day on." She worked in the abbey's library and at other tasks that helped to support the community financially. Beginning in 1965, she also served as the abbey's sacristan.

More and more she was formed by the liturgy. Especially in the Mass she found meaning to the question of suffering in the world. She became an instructor of the novices, wrote about symbols for the *Encyclopedia of Antiquity and Christianity,* edited the records of conferences led by Odo Casel, OSB, and later assisted in the publication of his literary works. She turned some of her entries in the *Encyclopedia of Antiquity and Christianity* into essays that appeared in various journals of liturgical scholarship.

In 1960, she began to write *Key to the Cosmos,* the work from which this book is excerpted and translated. As a disciple of Odo Casel, a spiritual adviser of the community and a key figure in the liturgical reform movement, she wanted to present a christological view of creation. For years she had studied early and late theology, the Bible, Christian antiquity, the writings of the Fathers of the church, and the religious convictions and practices of pagan cultures and civilizations since ancient times, as well as poetry, folk legends and fairy tales that were pertinent to her subject. It took her six years to complete the two volumes—adding up to more than 1200 pages!—of this comprehensive study of symbolism. It was published in 1966.

She had hardly finished this monumental work when she was asked to take on a new task. The Abbot-Herwegen-Institute of Maria Laach planned a new edition of the 15 volumes of the *Yearbook of the Science of Liturgy* published between 1921 and 1941 under the editorship of Odo Casel. The volumes required an index. The Institute asked the Herstelle community to assist in its preparation. The sisters agreed and assigned most of the work to Sister Photina. For the next ten years she spent every free minute on this complicated chore, completing it in 1976.

In 1982 a monk from Maria Laach presented her with the volume containing the index. The same year she became gravely ill, and in spite of aggressive treatment her condition gradually worsened. When she was told that her condition was terminal, she replied, "I am full of joy. I am full of joy." She died in the spring of 1983 in the abbey's infirmary.

—Heinz R. Kuehn

PART ONE

VINE AND VINEYARD GRAPE AND WINEPRESS

PRELUDES TO THE GOSPELS

According to an old Jewish tradition that found its way into early Christian legends, the Tree of Knowledge in paradise was a grapevine. As such it was very likely expressed in art as a wooden cross entwined by vines. This image is less surprising when we learn that a Roman author reported that the ancients designated vines as trees because of their size. Unpruned, vines could indeed grow to an enormous size.

The materials used to construct certain ancient temples testify to the massive proportions of these vines. Some temples rested on pillars made of the wood of vines, and Pliny wrote that the steps of the temple dedicated to Diana at Ephesus were made of a single vine from Cyprus.[1]

The ancients saw the vine as the equal partner of the Garden of Eden's Tree of Life. In the apocryphal *Apocalypse of Baruch,* the waters of the flood invaded paradise and destroyed everything that was flowering in Eden. The flood uprooted and swept away the vine in the center of the garden. After the floodwaters diminished, Noah found the vine and was instructed by God to replant it. Thus Noah became the vinegrower of the new world. Legend has it that he planted the vine at the summit and center of the earth.

It is no mere coincidence that, according to ancient tradition, that same spot is identified as the center of the lost paradise and as the place where Adam was created, where he disobeyed God's command and where he was buried. The rock of Golgotha was also said to be located there. It was there, too, at the earth's summit and center, that an angel was said to have put a seed from the forbidden Tree of Death into the mouth of the dead primordial father, Adam. Over Adam's skull would stand, in the fullness of time, the cross of the Savior — the Tree of Death wondrously transformed into the Wood of Life. The wood of the cross, according to pious faith, came from the tree of the Garden of Eden.[2]

In the view of the ancients who were conscious of the symbolism of everything they saw, sign and reality met in this center of the world. There Noah, as a prefiguration of the coming carrier of salvation, planted the vine of paradise. There too the blood of Christ flowed down like the juice of a crushed grape into the soil that hid the skull of Adam. And there the first-born of the new vineyard later grew from the true vine — the wood of the cross.

The *Apocalypse of Baruch* says:

> That which is bitter in the cursed vine turns into sweetness; the curse becomes a blessing. What is harvested from it turns into the blood of God. And as the human race had been condemned by it, so now does humanity, through and in Jesus Christ — Emmanuel, God-with-us — receive its call to enter Paradise.[3]

Deep wisdom and truth rest at the bottom of these rivulets of scriptural interpretation, which have justifiably been called resonances of the prophets and preludes to the gospels. What fascinates us here is the prelude to the unity of vine and cross.

The symbolic unity of Eden's vine with the cross is also hinted at in the *Martyrdom of Matthew*, an early apocryphal legend of the apostles. According to this text, the primordial tree of paradise was resurrected in the grape-laden "miracle tree." It sprouted from the sprig which the apostle Matthew had received from the hand of Jesus and had planted in accordance with the divine mission. This new vine-entwined Tree of Life, from whose top drips honey and out of whose roots gushes the water of life, has features of that first Tree of Life. As such it is a symbol of Christ's cross, the true Wood of Life, whose fruit and living springs of water transform this wild tribe into a new creation in Christ.

These ancient stories sensed an essential point of this symbol: It was Satan's envy that made the Tree of Knowledge a means of seduction. And when ancient faith portrayed this tree, this good creation of the good creator, as a vine, a hint of its true connection emerges. The symbol of wine and the images it engenders—vineyard and vine, grape and winepress—has been called a "theme of love." It is no less than that divine love which planned and put into effect the work of creation and salvation.

This tale of divine love, and with it the history of salvation, began with the vine of paradise and became a heart-wrenching drama because of the envy of Satan, who again injured God's love. But this time the offense was the result of a human being's seduction and consequent breach of faith. This interpretation concurs with an old conviction of faith that says Lucifer fell because he saw or suspected the union of love, the oneness of God and humanity in Christ.

Significantly, the Satan-driven betrayer Judas is, according to the Greek liturgy, a "traitor of the mystery." Could it be that Judas' rebellious spirit suspected the choice of wine as an element of the mystery of salvation? That mystery is the incomprehensible attraction of God to the physical creation with whom God wanted to be joined some day in the mystery of the altar. Thus would humans cooperate with the work of salvation embedded in God's own divine substance. Did the devil fall because pride rebelled against the idea of this symbol, which in God's eternal plan of love formed and marked the entire creation—with Christ as its center?

We make such conjectures with trepidation. Nevertheless, it remains that Eden's vine began the drama of love which drove God to nuptial union with humanity and to a creation united with God as its royal head. It was at the vine that the serpent lay in wait for the woman in order to rip apart the close bond between God and the human race. Thus the theme of love began with a break of fidelity, indeed with adultery, as humanity betrayed the love of its own creator. The chosen "You" tore itself away from the eternal "I Am."

Ultimately, the consequence of this catastrophe was the awakening of another love, a love not born of the Spirit but born of fallen flesh and blood, a love which from then on was destined to be the dark opponent of divine love.

Not surprisingly, wine is also associated with this other love. It is transformed in this context into a discordant symbol, one in need of salvation—a symbol burdened with the ambivalent powers of life and death.

IMAGES OF REMEMBRANCE AND PROPHECY

Is it not true that these ancient preludes to the Christian symbolism of wine improve our understanding of the significant role played by the vine in the history of salvation? Do they not hint at why God let vines spread boundlessly from the heart of our earthly paradise and conquer the entire cultivated earth? Vines were and remain symbols of God's love for humanity. They speak to us of remembrance and prophecy, nourish us with images of mountains and hills flowing with wine (Amos 9:13). They strengthen us with the promise of a coming time of salvation. Yet popular understanding barely touches the surface of such images.

It is only with difficulty that we hear in the songs of the prophets the imploring courtship of a God who speaks to our hearts, a God who with images of luxuriant vineyards holds before our eyes the grace of being a chosen people. Israel is God's own vineyard, destined to produce sweet ripe fruit. Thus the prophet Hosea proclaims, "Israel is a luxuriant vine that yields its fruit" (10:1). Great is God's joy, for the hope of Israel has been fulfilled.

When the Song of Songs speaks of bridal happiness in the fragrant vineyard, it is a prophecy of the spiritual and nuptial unity of God and humanity.

> Come, my beloved,
> let us go forth into the fields.
> Let us go out early to the vineyards
> and see whether the vines have budded,
> whether the grape blossoms have opened.
> There I will give you my love. (7:11, 12)

Yet God's great love for this vineyard is betrayed. Heartfelt pain over this sounds in the vineyard song of Isaiah. In that passage, tones fresh as a gurgling spring mingle with dark and heavy rumblings. Delight, disappointment and bitterly accusing wrath ring out in agonized conflict:

> Let me sing for my beloved
> my love-song concerning his vineyard:
> My beloved had a vineyard
> on a very fertile hill.
> He dug it and cleared it of stones,
> and planted it with choice vines;
> he built a watchtower in the midst of it,
> and hewed out a wine vat in it;
> he expected it to yield grapes,
> but it yielded wild grapes.
>
> And now, inhabitants of Jerusalem
> and people of Judah,
> judge between me and my vineyard.
> What more was there to do for my vineyard
> that I have not done in it?
> When I expected it to yield grapes,
> why did it yield wild grapes?
>
> And now I will tell you
> what I will do to my vineyard.
> I will remove its hedge,
> and it shall be devoured;
> I will break down its wall,
> and it shall be trampled down.
> I will make it a waste;
> it shall not be pruned or hoed,
> and it shall be overgrown
> with briers and thorns;
> I will also command the clouds
> that they rain no rain on it.
>
> For the vineyard of the LORD of hosts
> is the house of Israel,

and the people of Judah
are his pleasant planting;
he expected justice but saw bloodshed;
righteousness, but heard a cry! (5:1 – 7)

God's love for this vineyard found no reciprocation; it had wasted itself for nothing. Thorns and thistles were the response to God's favor; the harvest was a bitter fruit! Because of this rejection, God's disappointed affection turned into judgment and curse.

Yet God's love is greater than humanity's infidelity. Despite the Holy One's wrath, God's mercy is not forgotten. The promise of eternal fidelity cannot be revoked. God's remembered delight — the hope represented by the leaves and the first blossoming and fruit of the people whom God found like grapes in the desert — cannot be diminished. "The remembrance which cannot be extinguished has the fragrance of the vine." With the promise of the vineyard, God again lures the unfaithful beloved so that she may love and follow God as she had done in the days of her youth (see Hosea 9:10; 2:15).

Such images of God's joy over this vineyard and of the bitterly disappointed expectation of the vintner permeate the entire prophecy of the first covenant. Jeremiah laments, "I planted you as a choice vine, from the purest stock. How then did you turn degenerate and become a wild vine?" (2:21). In Psalm 80, the vine, spreading out over land and river, symbolizes Israel as vineyard with God as vintner and shepherd. Its terrible devastation is understood as punishment for Israel's desertion. The image of the vineyard invokes the cosmic primordial tree:

Your brought a vine out of Egypt;
you drove out the nations and planted it.
You cleared the ground for it;
it took deep root and filled the land.
The mountains were covered with its shade,
the mighty cedars with its branches;
it sent out its branches to the sea,
and its shoots to the River.
Why then have you broken down its walls,
so that all who pass along the way pluck its fruit?

The boar from the forest ravages it,
and all that move in the field feed on it.

Turn again, O God of hosts;
look down from heaven, and see;
have regard for this vine,
the stock that your right hand planted.
They have burned it with fire, they have cut it down. (80:8 – 16)

These two images — the majestic image of a flourishing people and the image of a people whose redemption from guilt and perdition is the source of the psalmist's struggle with God — stand in contrast to the feminine character of the vineyard as Ezekiel saw it. For Ezekiel, the narrative becomes a lament about a guilty mother (Israel) who is engulfed by the fire of the Lord's wrath. Far from any source of water, she withers:

Your mother was like a vine in a vineyard
transplanted by the water,
fruitful and full of branches
from abundant water.
But it was plucked up in fury,
cast down to the ground;
the east wind dried it up;
its fruit was stripped off,
its strong stem was withered;
the fire consumed it.
Now it is transplanted into the wilderness,
into a dry and thirsty land.
And fire has gone out from its stem,
has consumed its branches and fruit,
so that there remains in it no strong stem,
no scepter for ruling. (19:10, 12 – 14)

This is a lamentation, and it is used as a lamentation.

In these and other prophetic images the love of God is attached to the vineyard as a sign of the union of heaven and earth. God's love is a holy, passionate and jealous love which, though bitterly deceived, is constantly renewed. It is a love which judges justly; yet, despite its avenging wrath, a deep and limitless mercy remains. Forgiveness and salvation are ever on God's mind.

THE NEW COVENANT

Those images that the seers of the Hebrew scriptures understood as images of a time to come were brought to fulfillment in the parables of the Son of Man. Remember, for example, the parable of the landowner who went out to hire laborers for his vineyard (Matthew 20:1 – 8). Again a vineyard! The image incorporates all of God's plans and works, from beginning to end. The use of this image by the incarnate Word thus confirms it as God's preferred image for the people and kingdom to which all the love and effort of the eternal vintner are devoted.

Leading us still deeper into the mystery of God's desire for union with his creation is another parable, a dark allegory, which the Lord told toward the end of his life. In that context it is clear that both the allegory itself and all the prophecy that had pointed to him since ancient days had already begun to be realized.

In that parable, a landowner planted a vineyard and cared for it as did the vinegrower in the song of Isaiah. He put a fence around it, dug a wine press and built a watchtower in its center; then he leased it to his tenants and went on a journey. When the landowner returned at harvest time and sent his servants to collect the vineyard's fruit from the tenants, they beat, stoned and killed the servants he had sent. Finally the landowner sent his own son; he believed their respect for the heir would keep them from inflicting evil on him. But the tenants also killed the son and heir (see Matthew 21:33 – 46; Mark 12:1 – 12; Luke 20:9 – 19).

In this analogy Jesus announces both the high point and the turning point of the divine-human drama that began at Eden's vine-tree. God's love endures to the very end; it dares the incomprehensible. The vintner of the eternal world fights for the fruit of his earthly vineyard and does not retreat from the bloody sacrifice. That sacrifice required the life of God's servants, the prophets, and ultimately the life of God's only begotten Son. The son in the parable who sees his own fate approaching is the sacrifice of the love of the vintner for the vineyard that is humanity. The One who became human is enjoined to complete the entire tragedy to its final consequences.

The judgment that was foretold in the vineyard songs of the prophets closes in. The parables of the Lord proclaim that it is near at hand. In the course of time and at the end of time, God's judgment will destroy everything in the vineyard of humanity that defied the divine effort and rejected the fruit. But for the time being, the first judgment has been vented on the eternal vintner's own son. The wrath born of God's insulted love and justice, with the terrible fire reminiscent of the prophets, seized the victim of the world's sins who was hung on a cross.

The son and heir accepts God's judgment in his own body. He offers himself willingly to the Father, who upon arriving for the world's harvest is given the account and the yield of the desired fruit of the vine. Thus the son heals the disappointment of love with the deepest answer possible: He speaks of the vineyard. In writing the account of the earth's indebtedness on his own innocent body, he steps in for his people and for the people standing before the gates of salvation. Nailed by the vineyard's tenants to the wood of the cross, Christ, the perfect grape, bleeds to death. That death becomes the offering of the sacrifice which reconciles everything, restoring the covenant between earth and heaven and yielding the harvest which the eternal vintner had expected in vain from his vineyard.

I AM THE VINE

To accomplish all of this, the incarnate Son, Jesus Christ, went to his death with his own testimonial: "I am the true vine" (John 15:1). He is the undeceiving fulfillment of the vintner's hope. In this word of revelation Christ acknowledges his mission: It is he who must effect everything promised in the images of the vineyard. He is the vine, God's new vineyard; he is the grape and the wine which flows from it; he is the wine presser about whom Isaiah, fascinated by the image, proclaimed:

"Who is this that comes from Edom,
from Bozrah in garments stained crimson?
Who is this so splendidly robed,
marching in his great might?"
"It is I, announcing vindication,
mighty to save."
"Why are your robes red,
and your garments like theirs
who tread the wine press?"
"I have trodden the wine press alone,
and from the peoples no one was with me;
I trod them in my anger
and trampled them in my wrath;
their juice spattered on my garments,
and stained all my robes.
For the day of vengeance was in my heart,
and the year for my redeeming work had come.
I looked, but there was no helper;
I stared, but there was no one to sustain me;
so my own arm brought me victory,
and my wrath sustained me.
I trampled down peoples in my anger,
I crushed them in my wrath,
and I poured out their lifeblood on the earth."
(63:1–6)

NON-BIBLICAL IMAGES

Before we attempt to plumb the depths of these salvific symbols, the apocryphal analogies of this circle of images should be mentioned briefly. The foreshadowing of the Lord's self-sacrifice was not limited to the first covenant. The pagan peoples also shared in the premonitions and expectations of the salvation coming from the true vine. Their mythologies contain some parallels to the events that occurred in paradise and which permeated the narratives of both the Hebrew Scriptures and the New Testament.

According to Mesopotamian tradition as interpreted by the Jewish Mishnah, the wondrous tree in which Gilgamesh found the "wine-woman" Siduri was, in actuality, a vine, just like the Tree of Knowledge in Eden. In the ancient Near East the vine was identical with "the herb of life." Babylonian writings simply named it the "wood of life" while the original Sumarian written character for "life" was a vine leaf. It is clear that Eastern wisdom interpreted the vine as a primary symbol of life.

Other sources paired the vine and the fig tree, seeing them as the two halves of the world. Together they stood for the cosmic whole, holding in tension its ancient division of life and death. "To sit under one's vine and fig tree" was in the ancient East a commonly understood phrase which meant "to enjoy well-being and possession of all earthly goods, even dominion over the world." Or to put it more simply, it means "to possess the entire world."

Behind this imagery stands the aforementioned symbol of the *cosmic tree,* which ancient faith already linked with the vine of paradise. In the Near Eastern view of paradise, however, the tree and the vine are distinct. The vine, in fact, remains a symbol of life, perhaps in contrast to the Tree of Death or else as an analogy of the Tree of Life in other cosmic stories.

The variety of interpretations of the vine and Eden's Tree are not particularly significant. Even if the vine became the tree of seduction, it was still created by God as the wood of life. The split between life and death first came as a result of the sin against the "undivided origins of the cosmos."[4] On the new Tree of Paradise, Christ the true vine would reconcile death and life, restoring creation to its original oneness.

ON THE WAY TO THE CROSS

"I am the true vine." This self-revelation of Christ is as unfathomable as all the other images of the vine. These words announce the granting of an endless expectation — not only of human hope, but also, as we already saw, of divine hope. The artlessly deep, lovingly serious allegory of the vine gives and demands the ultimate. In due time, the true vine will seal with his last drop of blood what his spoken analogy had promised. It is precisely for that reason that Christ insists upon the need for "separation" and "decision" in view of the frightening consequence if humanity again resists the call to grace by the vintner God:

> I am the true vine,
> and my Father is the vinegrower.
> He removes every branch in me
> that bears no fruit.
> Every branch that bears fruit
> he prunes to make it bear more fruit.
> Abide in me as I abide in you.
> Just as the branch cannot bear fruit by itself
> unless it abides in the vine,
> neither can you unless you abide in me.
> I am the vine, you are the branches.
> Those who abide in me and I in them bear much fruit,
> because apart from me you can do nothing.
> Whoever does not abide in me
> is thrown away like a branch and withers;
> such branches are gathered,
> thrown into the fire, and burned. (John 15:1 – 6)

As can be concluded from the previous chapter of the gospel of John, Jesus spoke these words not in the room where the evening supper had been held but later, on the way to the Mount of Olives. Thus they serve both as a powerful conclusion to the supper and as a prelude to his coming death.

The wine-become-blood is an integral part of the rite which the Lord initiated at that supper in sacramental anticipation of his approaching sacrifice of redemption. Having identified himself as the vine on the way to the sacrifice, his gaze, penetrating the eternal, reaches beyond the cross and mystery, and comes to rest on that last and permanent unity of God and humanity for which the ritual of the eucharist is the only way and means.

This union was clear to him as the deepest meaning of the symbol of the vine, a union he had to accomplish as the fruit of his sacrifice.

The vintner of the church is the Father, who will cultivate, prune and purify the vine, and it is the Son who will be the first victim of the fatal knife. But precisely for that reason the Son becomes the life-giving vine laden with the fruits of eternity. Through the cross he fulfills the eternal and divine idea of the vineyard, the union of God and the human race in Christ and his church.

IMAGES FROM THE FATHERS OF THE CHURCH

It is that same divine-human union which the Fathers of the Church also understood as the deepest meaning of the vineyard and vine. The parable of the vine and branches points to our "physical union" with Christ, says Cyril of Alexandria.[5] That understanding is confirmed by John Chrysostom.[6] It is expanded upon by Augustine who from that image developed his theology of the mystical body of Christ, the idea of the mediation of the incarnate Son between heaven and earth, and the notion of divine and human unity. Augustine writes:

> The word of Christ means that he is the head of the church and we are his members; he the mediator between God and the human race. The Vine and vines are of *one* nature. Because we cannot take on God's nature, Jesus took on human nature, so that in him we too can be grafted unto the one true vine.[7]

The Lord's Death

This divine-human union could only have been accomplished by the Lord's death, a destiny he embraced when he spoke of himself as the "true vine." His death changes the image of promise into an image of salvation which carries in it divine reality. From the cross flows the life-saving blood of the grapes. This blood reddens the freshly flowing water of baptism, fertilizing it for the rebirth of those who through the sacrament become members of Christ and vines of the heavenly vine.

"Through baptism you become a part of the holy vine," says Cyril of Jerusalem. "If you remain on the vine, you will grow as a fruit-bearing branch of the vine."[8] Cyril uses the same powerfully expressive word — "remain" *ménein,* in the original Greek — which the Lord, too, used so forcefully in his farewell address when speaking about our "remaining," our "dwelling" in him and his dwelling in us. It is precisely that indwelling which Christ wants to impress on us with his graphically descriptive words of the vine. The organic wholeness of those who are saved and gathered in Christ's spiritual body is a unity of such depth that, according to Christ's own declaration, it corresponds to the mutual indwelling of Father and Son in the Trinity.[9]

This then is the grace of salvation which the Lord revealed to us: The divine indwelling of humanity with Christ is not merely a somewhat remote analogy. No, *humanity itself is implanted in the divine.* The Fathers of the Church have given us rich meditations on this image of salvation as they sought to plumb its fullness and beauty. Thus Cyrillona, the ancient Syriac poet, says in his second Easter homily:

> Let us now see why our savior compares himself with a vine. "I am the true vine and my Father is the vintner." In the vine of his body is hidden the sweetness of divinity. Implanted into the vine of his body is the vine branch and sapling of our human nature. Out of the vine of his body flows for us the drink which stills our thirst. From the sapling of his human nature stream for us rivulets of grace. The vine is silent when it is being plucked, just as was our Lord when he was judged. It remains quiet when it is being gleaned, just as did our Lord when he was reviled. Its silence continues when it is being cut down, just as when our Lord suffered death.

Instead of the first vine that offered vinegar to our Lord,[10] the true vine sprouted for us out of the womb of the virgin. This is the vine that satisfies human thirst and bestows life. This is the vine whose drink consoles the souls of the sorrowful. And this is the vine whose wine washes the world clean of sin. It is the grape of this vine which at the last supper squeezed itself out and offered itself to the disciples as the testament of truth.

The Work of Salvation

It is no accident that an Easter homily is the context for Cyrillona's meditations, because the circle of images interprets the entire paschal feast of our salvation. The new vine makes up for the guilty failure of the old one and in so doing, heals the break between God and humanity by uniting in itself the whole human nature with the divine nature.

The echo we heard in those voices from the Gnostic liturgy has here, in Christ, its true origin. Adam and Eve hurry to him who is the vine of the new paradise. With their lips they receive the blood of the vine in which life and death reconcile themselves with each other. The fruit of this vine is the saving grace which redeems what their willful grasp for forbidden pleasure in the garden turned into disaster. The people of the church come running to the grape now hanging on the wood and to the cup of mystery into which that grape had at the last supper mystically squeezed its blood.

Through his cross and resurrection, heaven and earth again become one in Christ, the new vine. In him the new creation has arrived. He is the height, the breadth, and the depth of Easter. He is the reality which this simple object of nature proclaims—from the silent witness of the cut vine and the pressed grape to the trickling blood of the suffering Son of Man.

In the fourth century Zeno of Verona made use of the same simple and silent images in his grand perspective of the work of salvation. He showed how both the first and the new covenants can be understood in the context of this symbol of our guilt and salvation—how our entire destiny enters into the great transformation through the new vine, Christ.

Zeno saw this predicted in the vine song of Isaiah and in Psalm 80:

> Although limited by the inadequacy of our words, we are able to give a spiritual interpretation to the process of the grape harvest. The sapling that has been cut to a certain size is the candidate for baptism who has completed the prescribed number of scrutinies. The cavity into which the sapling is inserted is the holy spring of baptism in which those who were dead receive the breath of God and are brought back to life through its heavenly water. This is a true

mystery. The supporting stake by which the vine is being stretched and carried is the image of the cross of our Lord without which the Christian simply cannot live and attain immortality.

The vine fastened to the supporting structure indicates the height of the candidate's path and life toward heaven. The candidates will be fastened with fetters when they renounce the world and answer the holy questions with a vow, thereby being bound in a spiritual way. The severing of the superfluous branches with a pruning knife signifies the removal of all their sins through baptism in the power of the Holy Spirit. The purified wood of the vine's trunk brims with tears promising fruit; similarly, the eyes of the baptized shed even happier tears of heavenly doctrine when their eyes are opened spiritually. Soon the fruit appears. . . .

When the time of the harvest of the grapes approaches—that is, the time of persecution—all the grapes are torn from the vine signifying the seizure of all the saints by force. They will be led to the winepress, to the place of execution. There they will be trod upon by the winepressers, showered with insults, mocked, and killed.

Finally, the juice of the grapes will be squeezed out to the last drop under the pressure of the boards and the winepress. Likewise, on the day of judgment Christ, according to the commandments, will demand retribution for the blood of the confessors to the last cent. . . .

The martyrs will be received into the hidden rooms of God's dwelling, there to sparkle, transformed from human beings into angels—bearing a splendid light to the beatitude of eternal life.[11]

In another brief tractate the Bishop of Verona develops his favorite image in a few sparkling sentences. He shows how, despite the wrath of God's disappointment over the degeneration of the first vineyard, God's desire to be benevolent leads to the planting of a new vineyard:

> It is the church. God cultivates it through the labors of the ministers, makes it fruitful through holy watering, fastens it to the beatifying wood of the cross and guides it to produce the richest harvest. That is the reason why today from your ranks young vines — that is, the newly baptized, who have been raised to carry the yoke and are glowing from the sweet liquid of the crushed grapes — have filled the wine cellar of the Lord to the joy of all. God will grant that all of this also be given to you as you grow in your faith, through the Lord Jesus Christ who with the Holy Spirit is praised in all eternity.[12]

Christian Life

The whole enchantment of nature reflected in these images of the vineyard comes to life in these early Christian sermons. They also show the significance of such images of salvation for Christian life. From catechumenate to baptism, from baptism to death, the Christian life is to make real what those images of nature signify. Baptism, with its rites of preparation, is the mystical process of development during which the incorporation of the candidate into Christ, the true vine, is accomplished. Whoever has through these sacramental mysteries been implanted into the death and life of the divine vine must also give witness to the grace of having become a new creation.

Even without such extreme trials, each Christian life has its own harvest of grapes, times when the vines are pruned, the grapes torn off, treaded and pressed in order to produce their juice to the very last drops. Without the grape skins and the heart's blood, no one enters into the process of divine transformation. Such a transformation is the ultimate meaning of the vineyard.

In his commentary on the Gospel of Luke, Ambrose reflects on this attractive parable.

The vineyard, says Ambrose, is the image of our salvation. Grounded in the root of the eternal vine, the people of God rise from the earth, embellishing the entire globe. Like the vine they are soon adorned with fresh green raiment and budding blossoms. They, too, take upon themselves the mild yoke. The vintner is almighty God, the vine is Christ and we are the branches which, if not bearing fruit in Christ, will be hacked off by the knife of the eternal vintner.

Christianity, says Ambrose, is called the vineyard of Christ because it is sealed with the cross and its fruit will be harvested at the very end of the world. As the vine straightens itself up when it is bound, as it grows and thrives when it is pruned, so do the holy people of God become free by means of ties, elevated by means of mortification, crowned by means of the cut. And just as the tender shoot is grafted onto the growth of another root, so the holy people grow from the wood of the cross as from the protective lap of a loving mother. Moreover, the Spirit of God, sent into the depths of the earth and poured into our body, purifies with judicious pruning whatever is ugly, raising the shape of our inner personality to heavenly order.

Once the time of the grape harvest has come, says Ambrose, we will joyfully dive into the flowing young wine, heaping on our laps the mild grapes, and tasting with our mouths the heavenly gift. Then will we squeeze out with the trampling of good sentiments the God-given fruit—with bare feet, of course, since the place where we stand is holy ground, the tribunal of the holiest of holy thrones. It is there where the grape harvest occurs, there where the vine of the world is situated.

Already now the whole life of the Christian rises to its fulfillment in a hidden way. *Ave, vineyard of the Lord!* the holy teacher calls out to the church. You have been sanctified not only by the blood of a single individual, like Naboth who died for his beloved vineyard (1 Kings 21), but by the blood of countless prophets and, ultimately, by the precious blood of the Lord. He fulfilled the model of Naboth; the fire that had been prepared for his vines he extinguished with his own blood. You, vineyard of Christ, are planted forever by the death of Christ and the extinction of many martyrs. The passion of the Lord and the suffering of the apostles spread you to the limits of the earth.[13]

Life Out of Death

Thus these preliminary images surrounding the symbol of wine already announce the death to which the Christian life is bound, in the same way that the life given by Christ, the true vine, is life out of death. The grape ripens on the vine, and the blood of the grape becomes the new wine. The entire cycle is a parable of the redeeming passion of Christ, as Justin Martyr already showed in his interpretation of Jacob's blessing of Judah:

> Moses, the first of the prophets, said word for word what follows: "A ruler from Judah will not be missing, nor a leader from his loins until the arrival of the one for whom it is reserved. He will be the expectation of the nations; he ties his colt to a vine and washes his garment in the blood of the grape" (Genesis 49:10 – 11). This is meant to predict what Christ was to experience and fulfill. When his appointed time had come, Christ ordered his disciples to bring him the colt of an ass which stood at the entrance to the village, tied to a vine. Thereafter he was crucified so that the rest of the prophecy be fulfilled.
>
> The words "He washes his garment in the blood of the grape" predicted the suffering Christ had to endure in order to purify with his blood those who would come to believe in him. The garment of which the prophet speaks is the people who believe in Christ, in whom God's seed, the Word, dwells. The expression "blood of the grape," however, indicates that he who is to come will indeed have blood, though not from human seed but from divine power.[14]

Clement of Alexandria likewise sees in the biblical picture of the colt tied to a vine a foreshadowing of the incarnation and redemption. Just as Justin interpreted the washing of the garment in the blood of the grape to symbolize humanity united with the Word, so Clement perceives in the tying of the colt to the vine a prefiguration of the same miracle, the unification of our nature with the Word in the God-man Christ:

> "And the colt," it says, "he tied to a vine," while he tied this simple and unsophisticated people to the Word, which he symbolically calls the vine, because the vine produces wine as the Word does blood. Both are, for humanity, the drink of salvation: wine for the body, blood for the Spirit.[15]

Once again the Alexandrian teacher explains the mute image of salvation: "Then the holy vine made the prophetic grape grow . . . the large grape, that is, the Word who was trampled for us."[16]

The large *grape*—that is the cue the Fathers used to build the bridge to the prophetic sign which points toward Christ: "the grape of the spies," from the Book of Numbers. In that narrative, Moses dispatches a small group of spies to go to the promised land and evaluate the strength of its inhabitants and the fruitfulness of the region. In the valley of Eshcol the men cut off a branch of a vine which boasted large grapes. They returned to Moses carrying the branch on a pole between them (Numbers 13:23 ff). In Latin it reads, *ligno suspensum . . . tamquam crucifixum*—"hanging on the wood . . . just as if crucified."[17] Thus this narrative is transformed into a hope-filled parable of the Savior for whom the peoples were longing. Christ—the true *uva passa,* suffering grape[18]—would bleed to death on the wood of the cross for the redemption of the world!

"It is not unusual," reported Bishop Eberhard of Trier in our own time, "for the blessed countries of Asia to produce grapes of such extraordinary size that a boy can hide behind one of them. Some berries expand to the size of apples, and to this day grapes weighing up to twelve pounds thrive in these countries."[19] Early Christians understood the significance of this symbol simply by looking at the world around them. This explains the intensity with which this image spoke to the hearts of the believers. Hippolytus interpreted the narrative of this scene with the spies in view of the cross of the savior:

> The Scripture says, "There they cut a vine with its grape which they carried between two men." The vine is the symbol of the cross, and the grape hanging on the vine carried by the two men is the symbol of Jesus Christ, who hung on a cross between two robbers. . . . The two men who brought the grape are the image of the prophets and the apostles. Just as the prophets proclaimed God's Word among the Israelites, so did the apostles proclaim the crucified Christ to the whole world.[20]

Already in early Christian art there appear cross-like images formed by a large grape and the wood on which it is carried. This was a popular motif until the late Middle Ages.

TREADING THE WINEPRESS

Integral to the circle of our images is the image of Christ treading the winepress. The winepress is indeed an essential element of the vineyard; it is only because of the action of the winepress that the transformation which produces new wine can take place. The winepress is the boundary between life and death. What a parable of the world-changing passion, of the blood-squeezing agony by which our Lord and savior passed into his new life, giving us the gift of the cup of wine for the mystery!

Only from the viewpoint of the cross of Christ can the prophetic vision of the winepresser in Isaiah be understood. It is this prophecy that inspired the Fathers to unfold the entire scope of the theology of Easter—from the redemptive sacrifice on the place of the skull, Golgotha, to the end of time.

As Jerome explains, the comprehensive connection of chapters 60 to 63 in Isaiah—the glory of God bright over Zion, the joyful message of the anointed by God's Spirit, and the image of salvation and judgment represented by the winepresser—is not pertinent, as some believe, only to the end of time. Christ himself applied this prophecy to his messianic stature (Luke 4:18–21) and compels us to understand these visions "from the first advent of the one who brings salvation." It was, first of all, in the person of Christ that the visionary prophecies were fulfilled, both in the flesh and in the spirit.

At the end of time, however, the story of Christ will extend in its completion over the entire world for either salvation or perdition. This is how Jerome interpreted the dialogue concerning the prophecy of Isaiah about the Lord's winepresser. He imagines a dialogue between the Messiah and the angelic powers who see the king of glory ascend, bloodstained, to the Father. The angels are seized by terror over this incomprehensible event.

This idea of angelic powers being terrified by the sight of the bloodstained savior is foreign to our way of thinking. Yet Cyril of Alexandria explained that Christ appeared to the heavenly hosts not in his simple human form but bearing the marks of his suffering. The angelic powers shudder and are terrified at his rising because this one who comes out of "Edom" (Isaiah 63:1) rises to God with the signs of his passion and thereby offers them an incredible sight. The reason for their horror, according to Paul, is that the mystery of the passion and resurrection of Christ had been hidden to all generations preceding him.[21]

Therefore the heavenly powers ask who it is who comes from Edom stained with blood. Edom, however, explains Jerome, is not the name of a place. It is rather "the name for blood" *(nomen sanguinis),* and in this context it refers to the redness of the blood which in the second verse (Isaiah 63:2) is called by the same name: "Why the redness of your garment?"

As the prophecy continues, the risen Christ himself responds to the question asked by the angelic powers. It is to him that God has given complete judgment so that he may crush the power of the adversary thus bringing salvation and freedom to the captives.

Christ trod the winepress alone. There was no one to help him. Neither angel nor archangel, neither thrones nor dominions nor any of the heavenly powers assumed the body of a human being and suffered for us, stamping down and crushing the powers of hell. No, only Christ, the incarnate Son, alone! He executed the judgment by his own suffering. He alone was the large grape in the winepress of the cross — trampled until the very last drop of his blood was shed. Seemingly crushed by Satan, Christ became the victor and judge.

He executed the wrath with which God judged the whole God-resisting world. Yet at the same time he became the messenger of salvation and the savior of the world. For us he submitted himself to the wrath of divine justice — offering himself in atonement.[22]

THE CHURCH

Yet the meaning of the winepress is not limited to either the person of Christ or to the final judgment when the Lord in the winepress of wrath will crush the powers of hell once and for all. The winepress is also a parable of the Easter mysteries which permeate the life of the church and so frequently find expression in its symbols.

Ambrose makes this clear: "For those who allow themselves to be healed, the church is the winepress of the eternal spring in which the fruit of the heavenly vine overflows for us."[23] But it is the winepress of the divine wrath for the enemies of God who cannot be redeemed.

The church is the source of both salvation and judgment by virtue of the "mystery of the cross," *mysterium crucis,* operative in it. Thus in its midst, above all in the sacraments, the prophetic visions of the winepress of divine wrath become a reality. These warnings are found in the Hebrew Scriptures (Lamentations 1:15; Joel 3:13) and continue into the New Testament, right up to the powerful vision of the apocalyptic rider in the Book of Revelation.

Who can forget that heavenly rider whose eyes are flashing with fire and from whose mouth comes the double-edged sword? Behind him ride the armies of heaven sitting likewise on white horses and clothed in sparkling garments. The rider's name is "Word of God," and with a blood-spattered garment he treads for the Almighty the winepress of the wine of fury. On his robe and on his hips is inscribed: "King of kings and Lord of lords" (19:11 – 16).

The significance for the end time of the judgment hidden in the vine and winepress is already present in the mysteries of the church. Those who wish to experience the grace of the mystery must first surrender their own judgment. As Christ could effect redemption only by submitting himself to the judgment of the winepress in free acceptance of obedience — indeed, he executed it on himself by divine self-sacrifice — so humanity can be redeemed only when it too surrenders to the mystery of the winepress. Without the winepress, there is no new wine, no new life!

Augustine reminds us of the inevitability of this pattern. When people enter the service of God — in the liturgy or through a life guided by the liturgy — they must know that they have come to the winepress. They will be trod upon and pressed, not in order to perish but to flow over into the wine cellar of God. "Oh, that the last hour of our life on earth may find us as the church has given birth to us in baptism! And when the winepresser of this world treads upon us, we want to be joyful and it shall press out of us streams of wine!"[24]

THE VINEYARD OF GOD

With this image of flowing wine, our circle of images once again leads us back to the beginning of our journey. In Christ and his church the mystery of salvation which had been hidden since the foundation of the world was revealed to the angelic powers.[25] Christ and his church manifest what God intended from the very beginning by naming the people of ancient Israel, indeed all of humanity, "beloved vineyard."

In all the vineyards of the earth God saw — and showed to those who can see — the image of our human longing, the sweet fruit of God's own loving devotion to humanity, the bleeding grape that is the incarnate Son who sacrifices himself for the guilt of the world. And in, through, and with Jesus, God revealed the redeemed new people born of the union of love between God and humanity!

The Son was to make the earth again a flowing and fruit-bearing vineyard of God, a new paradise, in whose center stands the "true vine." The *Apocalypse of Baruch,* mentioned earlier, describes the beginning of the reign of the Messiah as follows: The visionary sees in a dream image "a vine from under whose roots a spring was still gushing out," and he noticed "how the vine was still growing while everything around it was a valley full of everlasting flowers."[26]

THE EASTER FEAST

It is characteristic of the early church's joyful understanding that it saw everywhere in scripture the light of the parables of salvation which the Lord has sanctified with his own words. Here, too, the divine expectation is fulfilled: It is the harvest feast which gathers both human creatures and angelic powers for the celebration of the new life which sprouted from our vine, Christ.

So this is life out of death. Out of the winepress of the suffering Christ we are transformed into the independence and clarity of an existence like that of God. Beyond all the seriousness with which the songs of the vineyard in the Hebrew Scriptures deal with death, the delight over the harvest of salvation which was born of the cross expresses itself in shouts of joy and rejoices in God's love over its victory through the cross.

The judgment of the disappointed vintner which the prophets had proclaimed is simply the reverse side of this triumphant agape, this victorious love. God's unfailing love took the judgment first upon itself in the incarnate Son. All those, however, who do not want to be reconciled will experience this incomprehensible love as judgment. On that great day of reckoning the Lord of all will send the angels of wrath with the vintner's knife to cut the grapes in the vineyard of the earth and throw them into the pit (Revelation 14:18 ff).

Alongside this dark depiction of judgment, however, stand the vineyard images of fulfilled hope in Christ. *The new Paradise is already here,* and in its midst rises the eternal world-tree, the light-intoxicated vine of the new creation. "The cross of Christ is the wood of life on which the ripe grape was elevated to great height," says Anastasius Sinaita.[27]

Similarly Venantius Fortunatus in one of his hymns of the cross writes:

Appensa est vitis inter tua bracchia,
de qua dulcia sanguineo vina rubore fluunt.

In your arms hangs the vine
which exudes the sweet, blood-red wine.[28]

The cross is the tree of death transformed into the wood of life; around it climbs the divine vine. Indeed, this nectar-trickling[29] holy cross is itself the new wine-tree of paradise at the end of time. Here Christ, the new Adam, the true Gilgamesh, finds in eternal marriage the "wine-woman," his church. She rests at his side, as Notker of Saint Gall sings in a sequence of Easter Night:

Look, O Christ, under the dear vine,
plays the whole church,
full of peace, protected in the garden. [30]

Note that Notker specifies "the whole church," that is, the church grown up to the full number of her members.

To this end Christ's word is revelation and summons. "I am the true vine," says the Lord. The true vine is the body of Christ, head and members, vine to vine. God, the vintner from the beginning of time, speaks definitely through the singer of the biblical Song of Songs: "My vineyard, my very own, is for myself" (8:12).

PART TWO

WINE

THE BOND BETWEEN HEAVEN AND EARTH

The images of the vineyard have introduced us to a great tension in the encounter between God and the human race. These images proclaim the original bond between heaven and earth, its disastrous break, and its subsequent healing, renewal and completion. Thus they guide us from the very beginning of salvation history to its fulfillment, from Eden's vine to the vine of Golgotha. And so, after a long history of differences and contradictions in interpretation, the vines of Eden and Golgotha are reconciled. The starting point and goal of this journey is life with God in all eternity. Christ glimpsed this life and made it accessible to believers when, on his way to his death, he told his last parable, the parable of the vine and the branches.

Christ's journey to death was the entry to this new life with God—both for him and us. That is what all the images of the vine proclaim: the new *life* which gushes out of the cross as a result of the *death* of the Lord. As the Easter lamb, Christ triumphed over death which had permeated these earlier images and he unleashed the possibilities of the Easter joy which these preparatory signs could only hint at. It is in the wine, the fruit of the vine, that this transformation is symbolized.

A SHOUT OF JOY

Simply on the natural level wine is a shout of joy. Of course, it also nourishes, fortifies, sustains and heals a person physically, as does bread. In the more southern regions of the world and in the ancient wine countries of the East (wine's birthplace), it is wine — not bread as one might suspect — that is the normal and expected offering at a meal. Unlike bread, wine gives existence its bloom and glow, making it the archetype of the sweet game of life.

Bread is an absolutely indispensable part of life, while wine provides that something "extra," a certain exuberance. Bread is the strength of the earth, and wine the fire of heaven. Bread strengthens us for bearing the burden of the earth; wine exhilarates us and allows us to forget the grim aspects of this earthly existence. Wine raises our awareness of being alive and rouses us to song, to poetic enthusiasm, fearless courage, and lofty thoughts. Wine empowers us in word and work — the custom of consulting with one's cohorts while wine is being served is an age-old tradition. Many things are decided "between the rim of the cup and the lip."[31]

Both bread and wine nourish and sustain life but they do so in completely different ways. Together they signify the whole of life, in its depth and breadth. It is for that reason that the ancients, who understood the bread and wine as symbolizing the world above and the world below, believed that these elements constituted the whole cosmic mystery. They therefore counted them as constituting "the antique sacrament" and as being "a symbol of the all-inclusive unity."

We are familiar with an understanding of wine that connects it to the happier aspects of life. Indeed, the joy of natural life is also a gift of God, a wave in the ocean of divine life. A life filled with laughter and fully lived — that is the spontaneous notion that the mere mention of wine arouses. When wine is born, it causes jubilation and drowns out the mute language of the suffering and dying grape.

The vine is cut, the grape crushed. Yet the time of the grape harvest and the feast of pressing the wine are occasions for jubilation, dancing and celebrating life. When the wine flows, people — in ecstatic delight — enjoy life and forget distress, pain and death.

The Bible itself confirms that this creation is a gift for humanity from the heart of God which overflows with joy and delight in life. "Wine has been created for enjoyment since the beginning of time," says the Book of Sirach. We have yet to discover the height and depth to which wine fulfills this promise of God. "Go drink your wine with a merry heart," says the preacher (Ecclesiastes 9:7). The psalmist, too, knows the power of wine "to gladden the human heart" (Psalm 104:15).

The word of God in the Book of Sirach states that wine enjoyed with moderation is not only "the jubilation of soul and heart" but also "the health of soul and body." The health-improving, strengthening and healing powers of wine (which also find expression in the parable of the Good Samaritan) were no less known than its power to arouse enthusiasm.[32] Countless renderings on vases from the hands of ancient artists clearly reveal that the grape harvest, wine pressing, and wine banquets were probably the most common reason for jubilant dancing and healthy celebration.

BLOOD OF THE GRAPE

Yet wine, especially in the sphere of physical nature, stands in mysterious union with and contradiction to its animalistic partner, blood. The "blood of the grape" is the usual name for both the unfermented liquid and for the wine itself, particularly among those of the Near East. Indeed, Pliny calls it "the blood of the earth."[33] Such an analogy of blood and wine is no mere word-play or fantasy; it is founded in nature.

Wine stimulates the blood-forming organs of the body. Hence, the people of antiquity regarded it as the producer of the blood and thus the source of life itself. Since time immemorial, the soul and life were deemed to have their very being in blood.[34] Thus, the Book of Sirach states: "Wine must be considered the equal of life." Such statements express the widespread belief that wine and blood stand not only in mysterious analogy to, but in substitutional identity with each other as the seat of life.

Of course, this conviction already hints at the vulnerability of the life which wine, particularly in the sphere of nature, represents. One cannot think of life without thinking of its opposite, death. That is what the images of the vineyard already have disclosed to us in their serious language. The symbol of wine leads us into the metaphysical depths of the tension between death and life. The ancients had a deep grasp of this tension; it is therefore no surprise that some of their cultural and sacred customs would find their fulfillment in the Christian symbolism of wine.

From the beginning of historical time, wine served as an identical replacement for blood. For example, blood donations for the dead were intended to satiate the shadows in the depth of the earth with life and to fortify the bond with them beyond the grave. Such donations were frequently replaced by the drinking of wine. Eventually the drinking of wine also replaced the blood offering that was a normal part of the rendering of an oath. This replacement is particularly important because the custom of sealing an agreement with the blood of the participants was universal in scope.

As time passed, the moderating and mediating functions of wine prevailed, and the vulgar blood-drink of primitive times evolved first into a drink consisting of blood mixed with wine and later into a drink of pure wine. Already in antiquity it was customary to seal a bond with a mixture of blood and wine. Instead of drinking pure blood, blood—either one's own or that of the other person—was mixed into the wine with which one toasted fidelity to the bond and blood fraternity.

SEALING A BOND

The report in Plato's *Critias* throws a light on the lofty thinking that is behind such customs. Using Egyptian sources, the Greek philosopher speaks here about the ten kings of the legendary, long-sunken island of Atlantis. Every five or six years the kings gathered before a high column made of gold, copper and bronze that stood in the center of the island in the sanctuary of Poseidon. There they pronounced judgment and consulted with one another over matters of mutual concern.

During this gathering they performed various rituals which ultimately led to a "pledge of fidelity." Plato writes:

> High upon the majestic column, immediately above the inscription that displayed the holy laws and the formula for cursing transgressors, the kings slaughtered the animal that had been sacrificed when an oath was broken. At the foot of the column they prepared a kettle of wine into which each of them trickled drops of his blood. Then, with golden cups, they scooped up the liquid and each swore to all the others, to himself, and to his dynasty that he would be faithful to the law, exert just dominion, and be obedient to the oath.[35]

The Romans called such a mixture *asseratum,* a word derived from the Old Latin *asser,* meaning "blood." As late as the last pre-Christian century a Roman magistrate, the conspirator Catalina, is supposed to have had his fellow conspirators drink such an *asseratum* in order to obligate them to remain faithful to their bond.[36]

Even its horrible misuse testifies to the essence of this profound idea. The power of blood to give life and unite those who consume it transmits itself to the mixture of blood and wine. Eventually wine alone becomes the symbolic substitute for the blood. Wine thus takes over the function of the blood: A drink of wine becomes the worldwide rite for concluding a pact. It also creates familial ties, strengthens friendships, forges bonds and is a sign of hospitality and love. In the drinking of wine life unites itself with life, passing the power of one being on to another.

More recent customs connected with wine, such as raising wine glasses to someone and wishing them health, continue the theme of confirming a union by drinking blood. Even today the symbolic gesture by which bride and bridegroom signify their union by drinking wine ultimately has its roots in the archaic notion of the blood bond and the various forms of its practice.

Mythical premonitions of the fundamental and essential relationship between blood and wine also provide the context in which the ancients, according to Plato, characterized wine as "blood of the earth." Plutarch relates that at one time the Egyptians neither drank wine nor offered it to the gods in friendship because they considered it to be the blood of the Titans who were annihilated when they rebelled against the gods. Legend has it that vines grew out of their corpses which had decomposed into the soil. Therefore drinking wine filled them with the blood of their predecessors, making people drunk and depriving them of their senses.[37]

This myth is reminiscent of the Greek tradition according to which people emerged out of the blood of the Titans. In that narrative, Prometheus, the god who created human beings and suffered crucifixion, formed humans out of a mixture of clay and the blood of the giants. Such mythical ideas ultimately rest on the word handed down by Pliny which Androcydes addressed to Alexander the Great:

> *Vinum poturus rex memento te bibere sanguinem terrae:*
>
> When you drink wine, O king,
> remember that you are drinking the blood of the earth.[38]

DIONYSUS: GOD OF WINE

Nature, legends and history provide numerous proofs that wine is often identified with blood.[39] Yet that identification always implies that it gives life at the price of death. That which is a gift for the recipient was first a sacrifice for the giver. In order to surrender itself for another life, blood must be spilled, and spilling blood is always a kind of dying, even if it is not death in the physical sense. Life out of death — that is the context of these reflections on the images of nature and culture. That is the blessed gift of wine.

Wine replaces blood. Indeed, wine *is* blood: the blood of the vine, the blood of the grape, the blood of the earth, the blood of humanity, the blood of ancestors and Titans and, lastly, in the faith of the ancient world, *the blood of God.* Wine's might, its life, its blood, its uplifting, inspiring, bewitching power foams in the juice of the grapes, intoxicating those who drink it, depriving them of their senses, and allowing them to be possessed by God.

The name of the god inseparably connected with wine in the Greek world is Dionysus. So identified are the two that it was common for the

Greeks to simply use "Dionysus" to mean wine.[40] Dionysus is the personification of wine and the incarnation of the power of life and death. Thus he is inseparably entwined with all of these. The god of wine is a fascinating and frightful image of the cosmic interplay of life and death which began after the first catastrophe. Dionysus shows the world the two faces of a "truth which makes one insane."

Both the ecstasy of living and the frenzy of destruction chaotically break out of the depths of his double-faced nature. He is at one and the same time the god of ecstasy and of horror. He brings death and resurrection all at once because he himself has tasted the intensity of life as well as death. Despite being a persecuted, suffering and dying god, Dionysus rises from his fate victoriously and brilliantly. The ancient Greeks were convinced that in the sparkling drops of wine they drank the tears of Dionysus who had wept and shed his blood in order to bring joy and life. "Dionysus has wept in order to still the tears of mortals," says the poet.

As wine is considered to be twice-born, so too was Dionysus. Dionysus-Zagreus, son of Zeus and Persephone, had been ripped apart by the Titans when he was a little child. They devoured his entire body except his heart, which Athena saved and brought to Zeus, who then swallowed it. With his beloved Semele, a Theban princess, Zeus fathered a mortal being, a second Dionysus. But when Semele, the earthly mother of the divine child, asked to see Zeus in his visible appearance as the Lord of Thunder, she was hit by lightening and burned to death in the fiery glory of her husband. Zeus, however, snatched the premature infant from the flames, and, sewing him into his thigh, carried Dionysus in his mother's stead until the child was mature enough to be born. Then Zeus gave birth to him once again out of his divine womb.

A mysterious union of fate and action therefore connects the "god born of fire" and the fiery wine. In wine the fiery blood sparkles, just as Dionysus was born out of fire and water. He was called to life by the flash of lightening, called to epiphany out of the depths of the ocean. So, too, the wine is moistness and glowing fire, wetness transformed into fire, a mixture of water and solar fire. The destruction and revival of the twice-born god who had been ripped apart by the Titans and reborn by Zeus, who was persecuted again after his second birth, and who died and was transformed into a new life, are mirrored in the life and essence of wine. The grape, too, is torn to pieces, crushed in the winepress; the sweet juice of the grape is the blood of the destroyed fruit, but out of the fire of fermentation the juice is born, so to speak, a second time and thereby transformed into wine.

Consequently, the sparkling drink is the most beautiful parable of fiery life that gushes out of the life and death of a god. Wine has the Dionysian double face: Drunken bliss as well as madness sleep in the purple or gold-clear drops that can either add radiance to body and soul or reduce them to tears and blood. This fiery liquid has the power to unleash death and life. It is clear then what is hidden within this potent drink. Lust and suffering, scorching heat and coolness, light and night, illumination and confusion, enraptured life and the whiff of death — all of what is lovely is married to what is horrible in the juice of the vine.

LIFE OUT OF DEATH

And so the Dionysian symbolism and mysticism of wine is a profound confirmation of the age-old conviction that *life out of death* is both the meaning and the gift of wine. To the ancient Greeks wine spoke of the dying, perishing god who brings life and abundant blessings to mortals at the price of his spilled blood. This was a god who despite becoming the victim of Hades nevertheless reappears year after year as the shining god of victory, bringing spring with him. Thus he is known as "the beautifully blooming god," the blossoming god, enchanting sight of resurrected life.

Because of his fate this bearer of salvation was revered in antiquity as the incarnate union of death and life; he was the *anima mundi,* the "principle of the life of the world" and lord of the realm of the dead. Moreover, he was related to the subterranean powers as the "one who was like the night," or the one who "roamed in the night." Heraclitus clearly identifies him with Hades.

In the cult of this god, therefore, the whole tension between life and death — a tension also characterizing the symbol of wine — opens up. Dionysian orgies are the dramatic, cultic imitation of the god's bloody destruction, as well as of the wondrously powerful epiphany of the one who is alive. They are a picture of Dionysian life where, in staggering drunkenness, one tumbles into the abysses of death but rises out of the grave in new glory.

DIONYSUS, A FORESHADOWING OF CHRIST

By now it should be clear that the conflicting personality of the wine-god Dionysus casts a shadowy silhouette of the true savior and redeemer. This often terrible and horrifying god anticipates a superhuman reality. Conversely, Christ also throws light on Dionysus. The incarnate God, after all, is the pure reality of a God among all other gods—*deus deorum* (Psalm 49:1, Vulgate).

All the deepest and the most lofty traits of Dionysus are true in Christ. They are realized to a degree that surpasses everything else because all things that are true, real and valid exist only in him, through him, and for him (Colossians 1:15). And so Dionysus surprisingly heralds the God-made-flesh, Christ, the Son of the heavenly Father and the human mother, the mediator between two dominions by virtue of his divine and human birth.

Dionysus, moreover, heralds the persecuted, suffering and risen God, the God who is "coming" until the end, the hero who reconciles all things. Dionysus, also known as "he who loosens," is a god of "the most blessed liberation." As such, he and his symbol, the wine, offer an image of what prehistoric peoples dreamed of when they longed for a true redeemer.

Dionysus, the god of the vine—whose staff makes water and rivulets of wine gush forth, who produces intoxicating fountains from solid rock and who breaks down hostility and mistrust among strangers—shatters the norms of everyday life. He breaks the barriers of time and space and generates the ecstatic enrapture of the dance. Removing chains and breaking locks, he reveals a vision of what lies in the future. He who is prophet and healer, "the delight of the mortals," "the joyful one," the liberator from sorrows—he, Dionysus, walks through the world of antiquity as a mysterious omen of the truly divine Savior, Christ.

It is Christ, the messenger of joy, who will pour the sober drunkenness and prophetic charism of his Spirit over the redeemed flesh.

> You touch with gentle force the spirit so often gloomy. . . .
> You return hope to those who are anxious and give power
> and strength to the one who is poor.

This beautiful hymn of Horace about the Dionysian drink and its mysterious power to liberate those who consume it from anxiety and grief is, on another level, a fitting expression of the gratitude of the human heart for the true gift of the God of wine — Christ.

Later we shall see more clearly that Dionysus, the bringer of wine in the Greek world, was in some respects also a parallel to the biblical Noah, who stood as the type of the wine-giving redeemer. Noah — whose name means "consolation" or "comforter" — is a prefiguration of the spiritual giver of wine, the only comforter who became the true Spirit. Noah, too, shows the sublime features of "him who brings salvation"; he was the first to plant a vineyard (Genesis 9:20) — the holy symbol of life and of the beginning of a new, unbroken time.

Those figures who bring wine and salvation in both the biblical and non-biblical realms are subsumed into Christ and ultimately disappear before the absolute reality of him who was born, crucified and rose again at a specific time in history. He became for the world a source of new life — the wine of mystery. That wine is his heart-blood spilled out in his sacrifice; it is the "tears of Christ," the *lacrimae Christi.* Until the end of history he is in the sacrament, "the one who is coming," who appears with power even though he is hidden.

THE FULFILLMENT OF REVELATION

Even after this rather cursory overview, the words of Christ must move us anew and deeply. He who calls himself "the true vine" speaks these words over a cup of wine and thus the wine turns into blood — into the redeeming blood of the Word-made-flesh. With his mighty, miracle-creating word, the true bearer of salvation takes the hope of the peoples and reveals a new vision of salvation. It is Christ alone who is able to unveil that which has been hidden because only the true and real God has the power to make a promise and to fulfill what is promised.

In the world of the Hebrew Scriptures, the fruit of the vine had a holy function at meals and sacrifices. Both during the daily sacrifices in the morning and evening (Exodus 29:38 – 41; Sirach 50:15) and as part of the burnt offerings of the sacrifices for peace (Numbers 15:2 – 15), the wine, paired with the blood of the lamb or of other animals, becomes the sacrificial oblation in the exchange between heaven and earth. The wine is the secret ally of the blood whose enormous flow prefigures the coming magnificent reconciliation between God and the people.

This same alliance between the wine and the blood, along with its potential for reconciliation, was probably inherent in the use of wine during the ritual of the Passover meal. The wine was added to the roasted lamb, the unleavened bread and the bitter herbs.[41] The prayer before the first of the four cups of wine developed out of an old tradition of Israel: "Praise to you, Lord, our God, king of the world, who created the fruit of the vine."[42] Our images of the vineyard have already shown how deeply the symbol of wine was interwoven with the salvation of God's people as a sign of the everlasting covenant that bound them together.

Thus Christ at the Last Supper fulfills what heaven and earth had so long anticipated. He shares the wine that has become God's blood and which therefore has the power to unite God and humanity in a new and eternal covenant. The third cup of wine which was blessed and shared after the Passover meal became the cup of salvation in the hand of the one who made atonement. Over this "cup of blessing" (1 Corinthians 10:16) Christ spoke the words of benediction and transubstantiation that elevated the ancient symbol of wine to the divine realization of salvation. "This is my blood of the covenant, which is poured out for many for the forgiveness of sins" (Matthew 26:28).

The universal understanding that blood effects the most powerful bond and that it must flow where a bond is to be established was also deeply rooted in the worldview of the Hebrew Scriptures. It was a fundamental aspect of its revelation of God and the tradition of faith. The words of Jesus, "This is the blood of my covenant," are related to words and events in the

Book of Exodus. That which Christ consummates with his words over the cup is virtually the revival of the formation of the covenant at the foot of Mount Sinai. The sacrificial blood of slaughtered animals pointed toward a higher victim of the slaughter. Moses took one half of the blood at Sinai and poured it into basins. He then dashed that portion against the altar which here represented the abode of the Lord, the invisible partner of the covenant. With the other half the prophet sprinkled the earthly partners, the people, who had committed themselves to the law as written in the book of the covenant, and said, "See the blood of the covenant that the Lord has made with you in accordance with all these words" (Exodus 24:6 – 8).

THE OLD AND THE NEW COVENANT: A SYNOPSIS

As the first covenant was established by blood at Sinai, so the new covenant was initiated by blood on Golgotha, yet not by the blood of slaughtered animals but by the holy and pure blood of the incarnate God that flowed from the cross, the blood-sprinkled altar of the new covenant! This mystical image of the altar is the table of the Last Supper, as is every other altar of the Christian celebration of Christ's sacrifice. The blood that was to be squeezed out of his tortured flesh in the winepress of the cross on the eve of the feast of Passover was the same blood that Christ offered *in mysterio* to his table companions at the Last Supper in the transformed wine of the "cup of blessing."

Here it is significant that the word *haîma* in the New Testament denotes the spilled blood; it is an image of the violently destroyed life, a foreshadowing of the death of Christ. For those of the Hebrew Scriptures and for the Greeks, spilling blood meant the same as killing. The sayings about the blood of Christ in the New Testament refer not to biological matter but to spilled, flowing blood which symbolizes the violently annihilated life. *Haîma* is another name for the "death of Christ in its significance as salvation."

This death of Christ, while a murderous act of Satan and his followers, was at the same time the free surrender in love by the incarnate Son of God. This sacrifice became the cornerstone of the new covenant. It eliminated the age-old barrier between God and humanity and brought about a new relationship, one in which the partners in the covenant lovingly face each other, willingly work with one another, and are, in fact, united with each other. This relationship fulfills the promise the Lord had made through the mouth of the prophets (especially Jeremiah 31:31ff) and that had been evoked ages and ages ago by all the images of the vineyard. "This cup that is poured out for you is the new covenant in my blood" (Luke 22:20).

Consider how Cyrillona, an early Christian writer, describes what happened at that Passover meal, especially with regard to the wine, "the crown of all fruit."[43] He gives us a glimpse of early Christian theology with its synopsis of the Hebrew Scriptures and the New Testament and its images of a cultic sacrifice similar to those found in the Letter to the Hebrews:

> Our Lord first sacrificed his body himself, and only then was he sacrificed by people. He squeezed his blood into the cup of redemption and only then did the people squeeze it out on the cross. Before this occurred, he offered himself as priest so that those strangers would not perform the office of priesthood on him. He connected the mysteries like a necklace of pearls and hung it around his neck; he held the parables to his breast like a precious emerald, and with the jewels of the images of earlier times, he adorned his humanity and stepped up to the sacrifice.
>
> On his head he placed the crown of glorious prophecy. He sharpened the butcher knife of the law and with it slaughtered his own body as the Easter lamb. He brought the people to his banquet and called the nations to his feast. Those who proclaimed the gospel issued invitations, calling out loudly: "Look, the king distributes the body—come, eat the bread of grace! You who are thirsty—come, drink the fire; you who are dead—come, let life be returned to you!"
>
> When Judas had left, our Lord rose like a hero, stood erect like one who has power, gathered the fruit like a farmer, prayed to his Father as his heir, looked up toward heaven as the one who had created it, and opened the treasures with might. His face shone like the sun, his members resembled rays of light. His will glowed like an oven full of live coals,

his thoughts burned like lamps. As creator he let his salvation stream out; as savior he announced his mercy.

He revealed what was hidden, what was coming and secret, and what had been prophesied. He dressed himself with the true priesthood and with the perfect celebration of the sacrifice. There he stood, supporting himself with his love and holding high in his hands his own body. His right side was a holy altar, his raised hand a table of mercy.

He seized his riches without having any need of them and mixed his blood without being thirsty. . . . His thoughts were like deacons, and his omnipotence practiced the true priesthood. He sacrificed and slaughtered his own self, he dispensed and squeezed out his life-giving blood. He completed what he had desired, and accomplished what he had longed for. . . .

Come, my beloved, drink my blood which is the blood of the new covenant! Drink the cup of the flame, the blood that ignites all who drink it! This is the cup with which the first Adam was comforted in all his hardships. This is the cup through which the blood of the sacrificial animals on earth is being replaced. This is the blood through which body and soul will be divinely made holy. This is the cup that appeared out of the cup of Joseph when he used it to prophesy (Genesis 44:5). This is the cup through which peace and harmony between heaven and earth will be made. This is the cup in which mercy and judgment, life and death are hidden. This is the blood for whose sake God will come and demand the blood of his beloved from those who spilled it. Therefore, take this cup and drink from it so that you forget your sufferings; let it make you drunk and obtain hidden strength so that you don't flinch when you face your persecutors! Drink from it and eagerly drench from it the whole of creation! Through its power you will trample down serpents and by receiving it you will conquer death.[44]

In Cyrillona's Easter homily, the Christian Passover feast which had been sacramentally anticipated at the Last Supper takes on a new dimension; its relationship to the fullness of time and the expectation of final glory are revealed. As high priest of the divine sacrificial slaughter, Christ completes the mysteries of salvation contained in the law and the prophets. The ancient parables and archetypes surround him like precious jewelry. They come together in him who is the reality to which they point. The cup of blessing in the hand of the Lord carries the blood of the true Easter lamb. This holy blood accomplishes the work for which the blood of the lamb served as a prophetic model: redemption, liberation, rescue and the renewal of the covenant with God.

God's Easter lamb slaughters his own body in this first celebration of the eucharist so that he could surrender to his murderous executioners in the freedom of love. In this way, the blood of the lamb and the blood of the grape become one—the one true blood of salvation in Christ. He is the lamb that spills its blood, and he is the grape that squeezes its own blood into the cup of blessing. Already at this first eucharist he fills the cup with the blood that the brutal executioners pressed out of him on the wood of the cross. This wine, transformed into God's blood, is the drink of fire that was foreshadowed in all the heavenly and earthly drinks of ecstasy, the drink that causes the true, divine drunkenness of the spirit.

All that the Jews and pagans surmised about the purifying and atoning power of blood comes to fullness in the sacrificial offering (Hebrews 9:22). It is truly and fundamentally the *blood of God,* life and death in miraculous embrace, the drink of life rising out of the dying of God. It is the blood of "him who loosens," the true Dionysus, which breaks the chains of an age-old feud. And it is the source of redemption—a redemption which is "not granted, however, without the shedding of blood" (Hebrews 9:22). The blood calls the new world into life and confers immortality upon the living and the dead. "No other blood can truly sanctify." As the blood of the eternal sacrifice of peace, it establishes reconciliation between heaven and earth, invalidating all previous sacrifices by fulfilling their symbolic meaning (Hebrews 9:19ff). And this new wine was the consolation of Adam and Eve's descendants, from generation to generation. It appeared mysteriously in the salutary deeds of prophetic figures such as Noah, Melchizedek,[45] Joseph and David: a drink of fire that promised release from sorrow, liberation from suffering, strength in time of need, and victory over death and hell.

Such wonders are realized in the new cup of the covenant that Christ gave to his disciples at the Passover feast. This wine is the blood of the one crucified "here and now," the new blood of the covenant, whose "theme of love" deeply unites God and humanity, but not without the willingness of the human partner to surrender. The new and eternal covenant is consecrated in the blood of the victim on the cross.

The cup of the mystery is, as the Lord says, the new covenant, that which joins God and humanity in the deepest possible unity: "This is the new covenant in my blood" (Luke 22:20). The eucharistic prayer of Serapion of Thmuis, a fourth-century monk and bishop, gives witness to the same truth in a slightly altered version: "This is the new covenant, which means, my blood."

"DO THIS IN REMEMBRANCE OF ME"

At the Last Supper the Lord "celebrated with his apostles this great, terrifying, and divine mystery" (Theodore of Mopsuestia). Then he commanded his disciples and their priestly successors "to do this in remembrance of me," thereby establishing the mysteries and remembrance celebrated in the Christian cult. Note the way in which the words that instituted the eucharistic celebration are handed down in the reports of the New Testament and in the words referring to the bread and cup in the canon of all Christian liturgies.

A eucharistic prayer from ancient Cappadocia sets the context for the Lord's Passover, saying, "as he was about to go out into his voluntary and life-creating death." The liturgy of Constantinople, which emphasized the new Passover, says:

> As Jesus was about to be delivered for the life of the world, he commemorated with his disciples the Passover according to the law of Moses. In so doing he revealed the new

> Passover, in accordance with which we perform his remembrance as he commanded, until he comes again in glory. He took bread into his holy, immaculate and pure hands, blessed and broke it, and gave it to his disciples with the words: "Take this, all of you, and eat from it; this is my body which is being broken for you for the forgiveness of sins."
>
> He also took the cup, and after mixing water and wine, blessed, tasted and gave it to his disciples with the words, "Take this, all of you, and drink from it. This is my blood, the blood of the new covenant, which will be poured out for many for the forgiveness of sins. Do this until I come! Because as often as you eat this bread and drink this cup you carry out the remembrance of my death."

With the instruction to "do this until I come," Christ bestowed upon his disciples the power to do what he had just done: to enter into the mystery of his redeeming death, his new Passover.

According to the Letter to the Hebrews (11:28), this Passover is simply the "sprinkling of the blood" of the savior, just as once the blood of the lamb on the doorposts of the Israelites was the symbol for the Passover. The cup of blessing is therefore the quintessence of the sacrificial slaughtering of Christ and consequently of the whole mystery of the sacrifice, so much so that Justin Martyr and Tertullian could talk about the celebration of the eucharist simply as a "remembrance of his blood."[46]

It is a remembrance, though, not only in the sense of a subjective recollection, but in the ritually real sense of an effective memory that exerts presence. The holy wine *is* the blood of Christ because it is his ritual symbol, a symbol of remembrance. This humble gift of creation, "the fruit of the vine," is by virtue of divine blessing and consecration the mediator of the covenant of redemption. Indeed, it is the very "covenant in the blood of Christ," a sacramental image that in each celebration of the mystery binds believers to the Lord's once-and-for-all sacrifice on the cross, intimately incorporating them into his dying and rising.

Thus the wine of the eucharist, as too the bread, truly stands in the center of the ritual realization of salvation; human salvation occurs through mediating species, *mediantibus specibus.* Through the incomprehensible desire of the Holy One, the royal gifts of nature become instruments of the salvation effected by Christ; they are mediators between him who brings salvation and those who receive it.

Because of its central role, wine takes its rightful place in the divine hierarchy of natural symbols. In the symbol of wine the summit and fullness of symbolic meaning is reached, because in its very essence the wine becomes one with him who is at the heart of the meaning. Only in Christian worship does the wine penetrate the essence of the root words of symbol vocabulary in their concise and literal meaning—with words like *figura, typus,* and *similitudo,* Latin words for "figure," "image," "resemblance". No longer are the consecrated elements of the mystery subject to guesswork or modification. The signifying word of the incarnate Son defined their meaning. Christ himself chose the wine to be a corporeal symbol of his blood. Elevated from its role as a prophetic symbol of a yet-to-be-realized truth of salvation, wine was transformed in the Christian mystery to the meaningful appearance of a reality, to the sacrificial blood of Christ.

And so at every celebration of the eucharist until the end of time, that same "terrifying, grand and divine mystery" of the Last Supper is repeated in fulfillment of the Lord's command: "He entrusted to his disciples the celebration of the mysteries of his body and blood. He takes bread, he gives the body; he receives the wine, he dispenses the blood."

This wine is the blood of the true vine which flowed on the cross, the blood of salvation about which the Syrian liturgy professes: "The blood of our Lord Jesus Christ now flows over Golgotha and cries out to heaven." The eucharistic wine *is* the blood of him who redeemed the world, participating in the essence of the wine and united with it in such away that it becomes mystically, truly, and effectively identical with it—*vi verborum,* "through the power of the words" of Christ, as the Council of Trent says.[47]

Of course, only faith can see the miracle. The physical eye merely perceives the natural object, the *form* of the symbol. Faith penetrates what is apparent to the senses, disclosing the invisible, substantial reality. The words spoken over the cup in the canon of the Mass express it succinctly: "This is the cup of my blood, the blood of the new and everlasting covenant." The carnal eye sees wine, the earthly senses take a sip and enjoy the aroma of the drink made of the grapes, but the eyes of faith see blood and the inner senses taste the flower of the spiritual vessel — the Spirit of the risen Christ released from the cross.

In his First Letter to the Corinthians, Paul forcefully reminds believers of the unprecedented but demanding truth of this sacramental covenant with Christ. Because the Corinthians were pagans who had converted to Christianity, they knew from their previous religious practices that participation in the sacrificial meal accomplishes communion with God. Therefore in the midst of all the poignancy with which Paul points out what separates the pagan and the Christian sacrificial meals, he also refers to the evident analogy of the ideas governing the two meals: "The cup of blessing that we bless, is it not a sharing in the blood of Christ? . . . No, I imply that what pagans sacrifice, they sacrifice to demons and not to God. I do not want you to be partners with demons. You cannot drink the cup of the Lord and the cup of demons" (10:16, 20f).

The early Christian martyrs gave witness with their blood to the deadly seriousness of such sacrifices for both pagans and believers. If, from the pagan perspective, the sacrifice had been empty of meaning, one would not have to risk one's life in renouncing it. For that reason the early Christians stood with their entire being in the relentless tension between God and demonism. The cultic symbolism of sacrificial eating and drinking forced the conscience to a decision. Because the demonic counter-consecration raised the same claim as did the Christian sacrificial consecration — namely, that it united the human physically with the deity of the cult — the disciples of Christ had to renounce it even at the price of their own blood. Consequently, they understood that the Christian way of life, the eucharist in particular, demanded both a vigorous renunciation of Satan and all idols, as well as a parallel commitment to Christ to whom those to be baptized would commit themselves.

The eucharist deepens the foundation of the mystery of baptism — the most intimate union of life and destiny with the Lord, a union rooted in physical oneness. The drinking of the holy wine is a cultic symbol for this intrinsic union. Here its meaning is revealed in life's simple act of drinking to its deepest root, to the point where it touches upon the divine. That is what Christ meant when he hinted at the mystery of the eucharist at Capernaum and disclosed the goal for which the eucharist is the ritual means:

> Those who eat my flesh and drink my blood have eternal life and I will raise them up on the last day; for my flesh is true food and my blood is true drink. Those who eat my flesh and drink my blood abide in me and I in them (John 6:54–56).[48]

THE EUCHARIST: IMAGES FROM THE FATHERS

The Fathers of the Church attempted in various ways to shed light on the consequences of these words of Jesus, the cup of blessing of the eucharist is the true drink of immortality. It brings God and humanity together in the union with Christ, thereby nourishing mortal life into imperishability. Irenaeus makes this clear: Already here on earth, "the cup, the gift of creation" is transformed by the word of the Lord into a deifying drink of salvation. It implants into the body and blood of the one who receives it the seed of immortality. Already now the Lord nourishes us into resurrection and leads us — as well as the whole of creation — toward a transfiguration that will complete itself at the resurrection and manifestly new creation on the last day.[49]

Christ Lives in Me

The wine-become-blood is the realization of what humanity from time immemorial sought in its blood-bonds and blood-fellowships. Cyril of Jerusalem hears the confirmation of this truth in the promise of Christ. In one of his mystagogical catecheses he writes that the eucharist makes us "one in body and blood with Christ." Or to put it another way, it makes us "partners of his body and blood."[50]

These words summarize the divine elevation of everything that is natural. Those who receive the flesh and blood of Christ are united with him so intimately that they become one body and one blood with him — in the one body. Here the covenant in the Hebrew Scriptures reaches its original potential. In the same way, everything that the old world surmised about establishing bonds between partners, friends or between one person and another in marriage — indeed, even between God and humanity — was now realized in the sacrament of Christ's blood.

"In the form of bread you receive the body, and in the form of wine the blood," Cyril says, "so that you become a participant in the body and blood of Christ, one body and one blood with him. And so you too become a representative of Christ, 'participants of the divine nature'!" (2 Peter 1:4)[51]

Thus is humanity elevated to the nobility of the "divine family"! As the bread and wine become one with the substance of the human body, transubstantiated in the body and blood and life of the recipient, so the communicant spiritually becomes one with Christ, taken up and changed into the most intimate identity with him. This union is so complete that Paul can write, "It is no longer I who live, but it is Christ who lives in me" (Galatians 2:20).

John Chrysostom likewise proclaims with all the radiance of faith that through the eucharist we become blood-bound siblings, blood companions of Christ:

> We must come from that table like lions breathing fire, becoming terrors for the devil — fully conscious of who is our head and what love he showed to us. . . . "I wanted to become your brother; I shared your flesh and blood on your behalf. Again I give you this flesh and blood through which I became your blood brother." This blood generates in us the vibrant image of a king; it creates indescribable beauty. Yet it does not permit the nobility of the soul to wilt; it constantly waters and nourishes the soul. . . . The demons flee, the angels come running when they see the blood of the Lord. When this blood was spilled, it washed clean the whole world.[52]

Then, in a grand vision of the history of salvation, John Chrysostom shows how this blood of the altar of Christ had already been mystically present and powerful in its paragons of the Hebrew Scriptures. With a profound respect for Christian symbols, he declares:

> This blood purified the Holy of Holies. It expiated the golden altar, consecrated the priest prefiguratively and washed clean of sins. Without this blood the high priest did not dare to enter the holy room. When its precursor already had such great power in the temple of the Hebrews as well as in the midst of Egypt where it was spread on the doorposts, then more than ever was the prefiguration turned into final reality! . . . When it already had such force in what had been prefigured and death was terrified by its shadow, how then should death not have feared its reality! This blood is the salvation of our souls, with it our souls are washed, beautified, made aglow. It makes our spirit shine more brilliantly than fire, the soul more sparkling than gold; this blood, when it was spilled, made heaven accessible. . . .
>
> Since the dawn of history this blood was prepared in the sacrifices and slaughter of the just. It is the battle prize of the world; with it Christ purchased the church, and with it he adorned the church throughout. . . . The participants in this blood are joining the angels and archangels and the powers above, dressed with the royal garment of Christ himself and armed with spiritual weapons.[53]

In another passage the eloquence of Chrysostom, whose name means "golden mouth," is aroused by the miracle of the blood companionship with Christ in the awe-full cup of the mystery. He says:

> What is in this cup is the same as that which trickled down from the side of the Lord, and we participate in it. Paul called it the "cup of blessing" because, when we hold it in our hands, our songs call it by that name and we are astonished and delighted by this unsuspected gift. We bless it because he spilled this blood, his own, so that we would not stay on the

> wrong track. He not only spilled it, but let all of us have a share in it. When you long for that blood, then, don't redden the altar of the idols by killing mindless animals. Instead redden my altar of sacrifice with my blood. Tell me what could possibly make you shiver more than that? At the same time, what is more worthy of love![54]

This doctor of the church explains, moreover, how this blood is the highest proof of Christ's love for those who belong to him, a gift of his tender love for us. This blood is the witness of the sublime deed of love before which angels and powers tremble. In this blood the majesty of God unites itself with that which has been created out of dust, forming a community that not only shares and participates in the divine nature but actually becomes one with it. This is a union of body and blood, a mixture and fusion, a bond of such intimacy that "nothing, absolutely nothing, of an empty space remains."[55]

Nuptial Union

Scripture, liturgy and the Fathers of the Church understand the covenant between God and humanity to be the deepest meaning of the symbolism of wine. That covenant became a reality beginning with the cross. And it will last until the end of time in the growth of the body of Christ, the church, the redeemed people whom God chose as bride from Adam's original progeny.

Therefore this new covenant between God and humanity is basically and essentially a nuptial union, a marriage bond, a bond of love. It is the fulfillment of the whole mysticism of the nuptial union that already in the Hebrew Scriptures had been woven into the images of the vineyard. As we have seen, the theme of these images is fundamentally a message of love between the Lord and Israel. This message reaches its climax in the wine of the new covenant, in the cup of blessing of the eucharist, which is the blood that the Son of God sacrifices for the bride.

This wine-become-blood redeems and purifies his bride, the church, transforming and deifying her. It allows her to participate in the Lord's own death and transfiguration, and nourishes her with the life of the resurrection. Accordingly the wine of the "wedding of the lamb" is the mystical image for the entire paschal feast of the Lord, the feast of the new and eternal covenant-making in the loving blood of the lamb.[56]

Indeed, the mystical body of the church is purified in the blood of the redeemer. As we have already heard, according to the understanding of the ancient Fathers, the church is prophetically seen in that garment which the Messiah "washes in the blood of grapes" (Genesis 49:11). Origen, too, sees this prophecy fulfilled in the mysteries of Christ:

> In the wine of this blood, that is, in the bath of rebirth, the church is washed by Christ. We are buried together with him by "baptism into death," and in his blood, that is, in his death, we are baptized.

Those who were thus baptized are then invited "to the sacrament of the blood of the grapes," to the eucharist. After having first been turned into the "garment of the redeemer," they become — with ever growing awareness of the mystery — one body and one blood, indeed one Spirit with the Lord.[57] In this way the mystical holy marriage truly happens in the sign of the new wine, that is, "in the blood of that grape which — thrown into the winepress of the passion — created this drink."[58]

Fruit of Christ's Passion

The most precious gift of Christ's love for his church is therefore the cup of the mystery because it is the fruit of his *passion.* It is the cup of his suffering and dying which the Lord himself emptied so that he could offer it to us as the drink of life — both for our living and our dying. In fact, as Clement of Alexandria reminds us, "the Lord also called the completion of his own suffering 'the cup' (Matthew 26:39) that he had been enjoined to drink and empty by himself."[59]

Cyprian of Carthage, in his famous letter to the Caecilians, describes this profound relationship between the cup of suffering and the cup of mystery. In connection with the Genesis text mentioned above (49:11), Cyprian says:

> Concerning the verse about the blood of the grapes, what else could it refer to other than the wine that is in the cup of the Lord? Likewise, in Isaiah, the Holy Spirit gives witness to

> the suffering of the Lord, saying, "Why are your robes red and your garments like theirs who tread the winepress?" (Isaiah 63:2) . . . The wine is certainly mentioned not only so that it would be understood as the blood of the Lord, but also so that it might serve as a prediction of the eventual revelation of the cup of the Lord. Just as one cannot enjoy the wine unless the grape is first treaded and pressed, so we too cannot drink the blood of Christ unless Christ had first been trodden and pressed and had emptied the cup in order to offer it to the faithful.[60]

The word *propinare,* meaning "to offer," which Cyprian uses here originally meant "to toast." On the Mount of Olives the Lord, sweating blood in his mortal fear, took the cup of evil from the hand of the Father and emptied it down to the dregs in order "to toast salvation" to us who are lost.[61] Now, when he offers us the mystery of his cup, that cup is his suffering transformed into blessing; it is the death of the Lord who was crucified so that he might live in the symbol of the wine.

Because he has bled for the bride, the church, Christ can dedicate his blood to her as a morning gift. In baptism he purifies her with this blood and in the eucharist, he leads her into the innermost wine house, where he gives her his blood as the drink of life. "Look," says Cyril, "you hold creation in your hand, and the world rests in your love. Look, in your church dwells your life-giving body and your love, and with your bride dwells your holy blood."

The blood of the cup of blessing is the testament of his love for us "to the end" (John 13:1). The term "end" appears again in the last words of the dying Son of God: "It is finished"—*tetélestai* in the original Greek of the New Testament (John 19:30). This was the end, the completion, the ultimate dedication of God's sacrificial love. With this word the redeemer, having drunk from the cup of bitterness, once again reveals his love with his dying breath. In so doing, he poured from his pierced side the life-giving stream—the blood and water of the mysteries—into the cup of the bride. "From his pierced side he mixed his cup with the holy blood and gave it to her to drink so that she would forget her many gods. . . . It was he whom she drank in the wine so that the world would recognize that both, Christ and the church, had become one."[62]

The Principle of Christian Life

Christ and his church are one. That is the realization of God's great desire, *magnum desiderium,* in the blood of Christ. God and humanity, the Lord and the new Israel, Christ and the redeemed are united in such a way that from now on they are completely one: one body, one blood, one Spirit, as we heard in the words of scripture and the Fathers of the Church. The mystical consequence of this oneness is illuminated by Saint Augustine who teaches the neophytes how the bread and wine of the eucharist change the church and each of her members into that which they receive in the consecrated gifts:

> Christ delivered to us in this sacrament his body and blood that made us become these very gifts. We too have become one body and through his mercy we are that which we receive. . . . The wine was contained in many grapes and now it is one, one in the sweetness of the cup but also after the treading in the winepress. After fasting, after all your efforts, after humiliation and repentance, now you too have come to the Lord's cup in the name of Christ. You are the same thing that lies here on the table, you are here in the cup.[63]

The bread and wine on the altar are truly the mystery of our union with Christ and with one another. Like the holy bread, so too is the wine our mysterious image on the Lord's table, since indeed we become the body and blood of Christ — co-body and co-blood, as it were, with him.[64]

What happens here through the holy bread and the holy wine is something permanent. The message of salvation does not exhaust itself in the rite; it points through and beyond the sacrament into spiritual being. The ritual symbol is established by the Lord only for the duration of this time on earth. It ceases in the complete and lasting union of the heavenly world.

Yet the sacramental union with the Lord on this earth is only of short duration, and we would always be thrown back anew into the poverty and abandonment of "beings without Christ" if the sacrament did not give us something permanent, something that does not wear off with the species of bread and wine. The symbol of wine, however, leads us into that which is lasting in this union with Christ. It leads us to the spiritual Christ who, by virtue of his eternal procreation out of the Father, is the Word and who, because of his deed of redemption, is the Spirit (2 Corinthians 3:17).

Ultimately, the principle of life is the breath of God released from the cross of the transfigured Redeemer. It is this breath that believers receive as the fruit of Christ's sacrifice in the eucharist and it becomes their permanent possession. This fruit is the hidden sacramental communion of the same heavenly, glowing wine that the risen Christ poured over the disciples on the morning of Pentecost in an open, direct, and miraculous way. "They are filled with new wine," says the astonished crowd—and not without justification (Acts 2:13). "They were fresh wineskins," explains Augustine (Mark 2:22). "The new wine was expected to come from heaven and it came. And so we read in the scriptures: "As yet there was no Spirit, because Jesus was not yet glorified" (John 7:39).[65]

The new wine that was pressed out on the cross by piercing and crushing the grape is also the Christ of Easter, the Lord who is the Spirit. Because he also called himself the true vine, he is the essential substance of the symbol of the wine. The bitter cup of his passion became the intoxicating drink of his divine life, his wisdom and knowledge, his power and his effective word—hence of his own all-encompassing fullness. Concerning the event on the morning of Pentecost, Jakob von Batnä says:

> What wine is able to impart such knowledge? Rather it is the crucified, who with his wine inspired the apostles to speak. From him they received the new wisdom without receiving any instructions. Look, the juice of the grapes which the people pressed on Golgotha rises up in them and teaches them all languages. The new wine that poured out of the side of the Son became their teacher, teaching and instructing them.[66]

From here new light falls on the union of the Christ-mystery and the wine-mystery, both coming together in the symbol of the the wine. The same sweet new wine that on the morning of Pentecost intoxicates the young church is the same good wine that faith presents to those who are redeemed.

The divine wine of Christ's Spirit pours not only from the eucharist but also from the word of the scriptures. The revealed writings of the Hebrew Scriptures and of the New Testament are the full cups—indeed, in the language of the Song of Songs, the overflowing "breasts" of Christ. From them we drink the Word who in the beginning was with God.[67]

"As the heart takes delight in wine," says Hippolytus of Rome, "so do the Testaments of Christ give pleasure." Like children sucking the nourishing breast, we drink life from this divine well, because "the breasts of Christ are nothing but the two Testaments . . . they make those who trust him sober."[68]

The Banquet of Eternity

The ancient prophetic symbolism of wine, whose roots go back to the legendary vine in paradise, is here fulfilled, purified, and closely interwoven with the mysticism of love inherent in wine. Everything that was heralded about the grapes in the mystic and prophetic dialogue in the Song of Songs is fulfilled in the new wine flowing out of the incarnate redeemer.

Christ therefore rightly called himself the new vine because he is the vine of the new and eternal paradise. In him is secured the divine wisdom and knowledge whose power the first couple attempted to pluck for themselves in the forbidden fruit. They could not wait for the arrival, in the fullness of time, of Christ and his Passover on the cross. And now the breasts of this second Adam are the very wine cellars that are "better than earthly wine"; they are secret treasure vaults of the unsealed heart of God in which the treasures of wisdom and knowledge are preserved.

In fact, good wine already sparkles in God's word in the law and the prophets; the wine of Christ streams, as Hippolytus says, out of both Testaments. It was spiritual wine that the patriarchs and prophets poured out. However, what now comes out of the breast of the bridegroom is the superior wine that was prepared for the end of time, as the miracle of Cana foretold.[69]

But Origen also showed how the symbol of wine penetrated Christian existence with the realism of the cross. We have already determined that the wine of the eucharist makes a person a blood-relative of Christ, that is, someone intimately united with Christ's destiny. Origen now interprets the prophecy of the Song of Songs in a mystical way: The flowering and grape-carrying vine grows in the vineyards of Engedi.

Engedi means "eye of my trial." Step by step, the growth and maturation of the true vine, Christ, occurs in the depth of the soul of the inner person — from the blossom to the grape, and indeed to the sweet wine. First the lovely aroma of the wine blossom is mixed with the soul's basic elements; it is instilled into the foundations of human existence to strengthen the soul for the bitter experiences, oppression and temptations that will befall it for the sake of the divine Word. Thereby the soul matures to the sweetness of the fruit, until the mature soul is led to the winepress.

There, in the winepress, each soul experiences complete conformation with the fate of Christ. "There the blood of the grape is spilled, the blood of the New Testament that on the day of the heavenly feast must be drunk" at the joyful banquet of eternity. Thus the believer progresses in the formation of the spiritual wine step by step, move by move, until maturity is reached. In this way "those who are consecrated through the mystery of the vine and the cypress grape are brought to perfection and are longing to drink the cup of the new covenant that Christ took upon himself."[70]

In the third book of the same commentary Origen interprets the mystical "wine house" into which the bride of the Song of Songs wants to be taken (2:4). She directs her supplication to the friends and confidants of the bridegroom by whom she would like to be introduced into the house of joy where one drinks wine and where the meal is ready. Because she, having already seen the royal nuptial chamber, longs to participate in the royal banquet and to drink the wine of joy.

> We said previously that the friends of the bridegroom must be understood as the prophets and all who since the beginning of the ages had offered the Word of God. . . . All "come from east and west . . . to eat with Abraham and Isaac and Jacob in the kingdom of heaven" (Matthew 8:11). To this house and to this banquet the prophets lead souls, but only those, of course, who hear and understand them. The angels

> and heavenly powers also lead them there, because they are "sent to serve for the sake of those who are to inherit salvation" (Hebrews 1:14). . . .
>
> This wine from those vine branches remained in Jesus, not only on earth but also in heaven. . . . This is the wine for which it is desirable that all the just and holy ones become intoxicated. Noah, I believe, already envisioned it in the Spirit and, as has been reported, became drunk. And David, full of astonishment over the cup of this banquet, calls out: "My cup overflows!" (Psalm 23:5). Into this wine house therefore hurries the church and every individual soul which longs for perfection. The church wants to enter, wants to enjoy the lessons of wisdom and the mysteries of knowledge in the way she would enjoy tasty food and the wine of joy.[71]

In this mystical wine house, according to the words of Origen, time and eternity, the earthly and the heavenly, penetrate each other. In the house of the new wine the entire fullness of the mystery of salvation is collected and draws the celebrants into God. It is the house of the heavenly banquet of joy where the Lord drinks the "new wine" with those who belong to him. Yet the sacrificial meal of the mystery already reaches into the reality of heavenly eating and drinking, as was the meal prepared for the believer in the word of scripture. All spheres of salvation penetrate each other in Christ. Therefore the plea of the bride to be taken into the wine house of her lover is, according to Procopius of Gaza, ultimately a request "to blend me with the body of the anointed" — make me one with the body of Christ![72]

Sober Drunkenness

The Fathers hear a prophecy of this overflowing wine house in the word of the psalmist, "They feast on the overabundance of your house" (Psalm 36:9). Above all they find it in verse 5 of Psalm 23, which so often inspired the praise of the wine: "You anoint my head with oil; my cup overflows!" These words of David still echo for us in the Roman canon when the cup of blessing is consecrated: "He took the cup."

In the glorious cup of the mystery, in the blood and Spirit of Christ which it dispenses, all the prophecy of the wine is fulfilled, including that of its exalted gift, inebriation. Like wine itself, of course, intoxication has its levels of value and differences of meaning, from the animalistic and natural to the highly spiritual, indeed to the divine inebriation.

Already Philo of Alexandria recognized this fact and made it serve as an analogy of a higher event: the soul outside itself and experiencing union with God at the height of its mystical ascent. Philo turns away from the Dionysian ecstasy as a consequence of uninhibited material enjoyment of wine and instead turns toward a sublime, totally different divine inebriation, in which the power of the image of the lower drunkenness becomes a purified truth. For this holy ecstasy Philo coined the paradoxical terms "sober drunkenness" and "divine and sober inebriation." Eventually the Fathers of the Church, especially Origen, introduced it into the world of Christ and thereby into the splendor of its whole truth.

Indeed, it was Christ who first brought to the world the new wine that stimulates this heavenly drunkenness, the lucid inebriation of spiritual ecstasy that opens the heights and depths of divine wisdom, of hidden visions, of superhuman life and joy free of suffering. The sober inebriation of Christ does not know the tragedy of earthly drunkenness; it does not ignite the fire of the senses and the carnal passions, but rather the fire of heavenly love. It is the pure fire of the wine which "makes young women flourish" (Zechariah 9:17, Vulgate) or, according to the Septuagint, "breathes into virgins its aroma, its flower." The intoxication of this wine does not pull down but raises to the brightest heights of unwilting life. Unlike Dionysus, Christ does not lead to death by a life of earthly drunkenness, but through death to the everlasting life of eternity.

Paul knows this intoxication with the coming age and the new life that is already pulsating in Christ's members when he calls out to believers: "Be filled with the Spirit!" (Ephesians 5:18). It is this intoxication that filled the disciples on the morning of Pentecost, as it filled the prophets of both Testaments—indeed, all those who are seized and driven by the fiery breath of the risen Christ.

This drunkenness is also what the singer of the eleventh ode of Solomon meant in saying, "My drunkenness was not ignorance but I left the emptiness." This is not the drunkenness of any earthly wine nor the deceptive lust that confuses the mind but rather the divinely enlightening inebriation of wisdom and the knowledge which unites us with God. It leads to ecstasy and enthusiasm — a sense of being outside one's self and in God. Stepping out of what is of this earth and entering into what is heavenly. That is the gift of the new wine whose cupbearer is "the sweet-tasting Word who lifts beyond what is human. This drunkenness is not senseless but divine; it is being in God."[73]

In the West it was Ambrose, the enthusiastic disciple of Origen, who incorporated the concept of "sober inebriation" into the proclamation of the Christian symbolism of wine. This "sober drunkenness" is one of the favorite themes of Ambrose's mysticism. In his beautiful hymn "Splendor of the Father's Glory," Ambrose revels in the sober inebriation of the spiritual life:

> *Christusque sit nobis cibus,*
> *potusque noster sit fides;*
> *laeti bibamus sobriam*
> *ebrietatem Spiritus.*
>
> May Christ be food for us,
> And may faith be our drink;
> Let us rejoice to drink
> the Spirit's sober intoxication.

In his exegetical writings Ambrose describes the holy inebriation that the crucified and transfigured Christ pours out in his blood and Spirit over the redeemed flesh:

> There is also a cup with which you keep purifying your innermost spirit. It is neither a cup of the old nature nor of the usual vine, but a new cup that was brought from heaven to earth, pressed out of that strange grape which, like the grape from the vine, was hanging incarnate from the wood of the cross. From this grape is made the wine that delights the heart of humanity, intoxicates sobriety, emits the mist of faith and of true piety, and pours out complete abstinence.[74]

Exuberance of Graces

In another meditation Ambrose reflects on the threefold inebriation of blood, Spirit and scripture that is offered in the wine house of the church. On the table of the mysteries

> also stands the overflowing cup that is so glorious, so powerful. . . . Powerful, because through it sins are being washed away and redeemed. The inebriation of the cup of salvation is therefore good. But there is yet another inebriation, in the abundance of the holy scriptures. And still another in the outpouring of the Holy Spirit. That is why, according to the Acts of the Apostles, those who spoke in different languages seemed to the listeners to be full of wine. Consequently the house is the church, the fullness of the house is the exuberance of graces.[75]

From here new light is also shed on the mysterious figure whom Ambrose calls "the drunken Noah." Ambrose, as did Irenaeus and Cyprian before him, sees in this figure the prophetic image of Christ, the divine wine-bringer, the progenitor of the new humanity and the Lord of the world's new time. As the true consoler and redeemer of the seed of Adam, Christ gives divine inebriation to a new creation.

MIXING WINE AND WATER

After all that the symbol of wine has revealed to us about the relationship between God and humanity and its realization in Christ and the church, we reflect upon yet another image that is of equal importance, one that is highly treasured in the Christian tradition. It is the mixing of wine and water during the preparation of the gifts in the Roman liturgy. (In other liturgies, this takes place at the beginning of the celebration.) The habit of mixing wine with water no doubt corresponds to a universal custom, yet according to an old tradition its origins as part of the eucharistic preparation of the cup go back to Christ himself.

The Fathers of the Church liked to interpret the mixing of these two elements allegorically, as did Clement of Alexandria. He explains that God first gave the water in the desert,

> then the vine brought forth the prophetic grape. . . . The large grape is the Word who was squeezed out for us. It was the will of the Word that the blood of the vine mix itself with the water, just as his blood mixes itself for our salvation. The blood of the Lord is twofold: one part is corporeal, and through it we were redeemed from perdition; the other is spiritual, and with it we are anointed. Drinking the blood of Jesus means to participate in the immortality of the Lord. . . . This is a parallel to the mixing of wine in water, and to the mixing of the Spirit in humanity. The mixture of water and wine nourishes us so that we may have faith; the mixture of the Spirit in humanity leads to immortality. The mixture of both, however, of drink and of Word, is called eucharist, the praised and glorious grace.
>
> When we participate in the eucharist with faith, both body and soul are consecrated because the Father mixes humanity, the divine creation, with the Spirit and the Word. In truth, the Spirit is connected with the soul, strengthening and supporting it, and the Word is connected with the flesh, for whose sake "the Word became flesh."[76]

In the Roman liturgy the prayer—originally a Christmas oration[77]—that the priest says during the preparation of the sacrificial gifts when a small amount of water is mixed with the wine, profoundly and clearly illustrates this mystery of the union of the divine and the human: "By the mystery of this water and wine may we come to share in the divinity of Christ, who humbled himself to share in our humanity."[78]

As the prayers of other liturgies show, the mixing of water and wine is a reminder of the water and blood flowing from the crucified Lord's side. In the Byzantine church there is a unique ritual involving water and wine that presents another level of symbolism. Shortly before the communion the priest pours a small amount of hot water, the so-called *zéon*—meaning to cook or boil—into the consecrated cup.

The Eastern church sees in this fiery water a symbol of the Holy Spirit who, according to the scripture and liturgy, manifests itself in fire as well as in water. This mixture has the intoxicating power of fire and the purifying power of living water—water that nourishes with immortal life. In the fullness of life that encompasses all created powers it is truly a "fire water" when we recognize it as such in the order of creation. Are we not also touching here on the deep meaning of the sign at Cana, the changing of water into wine?

The cool, earthly element of moisture—an image of the mortal substance of creation and the transitory world—is here changed and transferred by the incarnate God into participation in the fiery nature of the spiritual which is symbolized by the wine. The fourth book of Ezra (2 Esdras 14:39–40) speaks of just such a fire-water of God's Spirit from which ultimately all the prophetic power of both the wine and water originates:

> Look, a full cup was given to me; it was filled with a water whose color equaled that of fire. I took it and drank. And when I had drunk, understanding poured out of my heart, my chest expanded with wisdom, and my soul preserved the remembrance.

THE CHALICE OF CHRIST

In their narratives about the Last Supper the synoptic gospels report a mysterious saying of Jesus: "I tell you, I will never again drink of the fruit of the vine until that day when I drink it new in the kingdom of God" (Mark 14:25; Luke 22:18). When the Lord spoke these words, their fulfillment was imminent. At the Last Supper he mystically anticipated their fulfillment; through his death on the cross, the fulfillment became a reality. And so whenever we "drink this cup" and "proclaim his death" we already mysteriously stand in that day when "he will come again in glory."

The paschal feast of the Lord inaugurates the feast of the kingdom at which the risen Christ drinks the new wine with those who belong to him. In each celebration of the body and blood of Christ the church on earth participates in the heavenly banquet of joy and in the cup of the "vine of David."

According to the *Didache* (9:2) the early Christian community gave thanks over the cup, saying, "We give you thanks, our Father, for the holy vine of your servant David that you revealed to us through Jesus, your beloved. To you be glory in eternity." David embodies the ideal image of royalty from the Hebrew Scriptures. Hence, the long-awaited Messiah would be called the "new" and "last" David.

The writings of the New Testament explicitly confirm the fulfillment of this hope in Christ by portraying him as a descendant of the house of David, one born in Bethlehem, the city of David. He would be known as the "son of David," the one who possesses "the keys of David," that is, the one who possesses his monarchy.[79]

Christ, the second Adam, is at the same time the new and last, the true and perfect David. As such he is the Alpha and Omega of the history of salvation (Revelation 22:13). Just as he called himself the "true vine," so in and with his church he is the new Israel — the fulfillment of the "vine of David." It is he who, according to Clement of Alexandria, "poured the wine, the blood of the vine of David, on our wounded souls."[80]

For us on earth, the heavenly drunkenness of which the Fathers speak is rooted in the fact that it poured forth from the renunciation and humiliation of the incarnate God, an act which was the origin of subsequent human adversity. Thus the gift of the new wine bound itself in graced analogy to the old law of the drink of grapes. This is reflected in Origen's statement that we "become intoxicated from the blood of the true vine which rises from the root of David."[81]

The vine of David is Christ the Messiah, the offspring from the root and lineage of the first David. He revealed himself to us in the vine and cup of David,[82] that is, he "unveiled it in its ultimate depths and surrendered it to us." With his church he is the "one vine" of the divine choice of love. In this oneness — the marriage of humanity united with the incarnate Son to God — the longing of the divine *agape* for the devotion of its creature is fulfilled. It was this longing to which Christ referred on the evening before his passion: "I have eagerly desired to eat this Passover with you before I suffer" (Luke 22:15).

He then took up the cup. This is indeed the cup of Christ, the new wine of Christ, which is the blessing of the end without end.

In contrast, the Book of Revelation repeatedly uses the sinister image of a divine cup of wrath. When the cup of wrath appears, it marks the extinction of the universe with its sign of terror. It is the wine-cup of wrath that the gloomy visions of the prophets saw descending upon the enemies of the Lord and it is this cup which the angels of God pour out over the doomed earth.[83] These images thus have a part in the multi-dimensional symbolism of wine. Their apocalyptic side, as mysterious as the night, belongs as unpredictably to the totality of the order of salvation as heaven belongs to hell.

God's wine of wrath is the eternal drink of death for those who deny their bond with God, those who reject God yet indulge in intoxication with the wine of sin and the cup of immorality.[84] The cup of divine wrath and revenge is, in a manner of speaking, the hellish, satanic dimension of the feast. In the wine of wrath the evil one and his followers willingly drink none other than the unchangeable love of God — now "changed" into wrath and judgment.

"I WILL DRINK IT WITH YOU IN THE KINGDOM OF GOD"

To the redeemed, however, this love gives itself eternally as the inebriating new wine of the heavenly assembly. The Lord's word at the Last Supper regarding this "new wine in the kingdom of God" brings us back to the roots of this symbol. God's innermost life is, as the ancient religions already divined, the primordial wine and eternal inebriation — "everlasting drunkenness," if we may say it once again in the words of Philo.

God's life is a life of inebriation. It is God's desire to draw all created beings into this divinely sober intoxication. Consequently, the basic meaning of all the various dimensions of this symbol, including its Christian elements, is this: In the revelation and communication of the divine truth and reality "there is no part that is not inebriated." Yet the road to this divine inebriation passes through the hard sobriety of the cross of Christ. He himself emptied the cup to the last drop in unmitigated alertness to human suffering. He also challenged those who belonged to him, saying, "Are you able to drink the cup that I am about to drink?" (Matthew 20:22)

The path to divine intoxication leads through the Passover of Christ—both for the Lord himself and for his disciples, his followers. Augustine said it succinctly:

> The grape is not wine . . . unless it has been pressed. So it is with human beings whom God predetermined from the very beginning to be of the same image as his incarnate Son, the grape who was the first to be treaded in his passion.
>
> Whoever enters into the service of God should know the inescapable reality of the winepress. Whoever is maltreated, crushed and pressed out is thus treated not so that he or she may perish in this world but in order that that person might flow into the beyond, into the wine cellars of God. As the grape is stripped of its skin, so will each person be disrobed of the cover of carnal desire, the cravings of the flesh. Therefore the apostle says: "Strip off the old self with its practices and clothe yourselves with the new self" (Colossians 3:9f). Yet this can not happen without the pressing, without the crushing. That is why the churches of God in this earthly existence are called "winepresses."[85]

Throughout the ages Christian martyrs have given witness to the mystical Christian understanding of the relationship of blood and wine. Countless members of the body of Christ lived out its meaning to its ultimate consequence. But the same is also true for all Christians who in the bloodless martyrdom of faithful lives "pour out the faith like blood over their whole lives until the end."[86] In this way the divine wine cellars will be filled until the end of time.

The heavenly banquet is attended by those with whom the Lord drinks the new wine in the kingdom of the Father.

The wine, however, that comes forth from the new vine is always new. The loving insight into God's knowledge and wisdom is always new because of the progress of interior experience. That is why Jesus tells his disciples: 'I will drink it new with you in the kingdom of God.' The grasp and disclosure of that which is secret and hidden is constantly made new through God's wisdom, not only for humanity but also for angels and the heavenly powers.[87]

The heavenly life is an endless journey from clarity to clarity, from light to light, from thought to thought, from inebriation to inebriation. All of this is one: the new wine of Christ, the new wine that since the six days of creation is being held ready in its grapes for the banquet of the beatified in the future world.

PART ONE

GRAIN AND EAR

SOWING AND REAPING

GRAIN AND EAR

When the wind plays in the fields of wheat so that they begin to whisper and sway in light-golden waves, spreading the aroma of ripeness, we have reached the climax of the growing cycle — harvest time. It is a wondrous time of the year. Why then does our mood turn so serious when we walk quietly through a field of wheat? Do we sense that the wheat, ear after ear, will fall inevitably, silently before the reaper? What is it about the wheat that touches us with dark premonitions and forebodings?

A PARABLE OF LIFE

In the natural cycle of the wheat's existence we glimpse the primordial secret of the fruit, a secret that seems to breathe eternally in the great cosmic rhythm of growth and decay. Once the wheat is ripe, the year has reached its zenith and the life of vegetation begins to decline. In truth, is not the mere appearance of the ear already a participation in this rising and inevitable decline? In its ripened state, with its blessing of fruit, the plant has attained its full height; it assumes the posture of readiness for death.

The grain has had a long history before it arrives at what is both a zenith and turning point in its development. It was last autumn when the sower walked across the land and spread the seed; autumn when the earth, prepared by the plowshare, received the seed into its dark womb; autumn when grain after grain fell to the ground and had to die. Year after year, that was and is the way it all begins: with surrender and death. "Those who go out weeping, bearing the seed for growing . . ." (Psalm 126:6). Yet out of annihilation comes new being, and yet the sower "does not know how" (Mark 4:27). As a "dead and silent body" the grain decays in the soil![1]

Yet when winter moves into the land, the seedlings of wheat already stand erect in green rows. Throughout the long winter the grain must endure cold and wetness. When spring finally arrives, the developing wheat grass provides glimpses of the coming abundance. Nurtured by the ever-stronger warmth of the sun, the stalks shoot up to a boy's height. And when the fine buds open, the wind does its work so that the blooming may be fruitful. Suddenly it is there — "the full grain!" (Mark 4:28). Then under the weight of this blessing the stalk begins to bow down. The heavier the grains become, the more the stalk bends toward the ground — turning the direction of its growth back to its source.

From time immemorial people understood the pattern which the grain follows on its journey toward its final fate as a parable of the path that is predestined for all of nature. The law of this path is the eternal cycle of decay and revival. In the heavens the cycle is followed by the stars; on earth by vegetation and all animal life. Fall and rise are the eternal pattern of life. This is clearly noticed in the life of the grain.

As the fate of the grain of wheat — so the fate of humanity! Indeed, they are wondrously related to each other. Ancient people already noticed this relationship. Our beginning is like that of the grain: with conception and birth from the motherly womb. And as the grain eventually decays, so does human life. We grow up, mature and then wither away. Mother earth waits for us — as both tomb and womb.

Thus it is very easy for us to consider an image of procreation and birth in the grain that the farmer sows, and in the shoot that breaks out of the soil of the field. A mysterious cadence unites the processes of vegetation and those of human life. Even today, graphic words from the sphere of plant life — such as seed, embryo, fertilization, fertility and infertility — are also familiar to everyone in the sphere of human life.

We can trace, for example, how intimately *child* and *grain* are related because of an ancient correlation of symbols. The German word for "wheat" is closely connected to the word which means "that which is being carried" — that which, like a child in a mother's womb, is being carried and born to full term. How naturally they are related — child and grain! Note the once common custom of "rocking" a child in a winnowing basket. Such a basket was used to separate the kernels of wheat from the hulls, the chaff. The basket was filled with grain which was then tossed into the air, allowing the wind to carry away the lighter particles. This practice cleans the harvested grain. The grain, when it is being rocked by the wind, is winnowed into rich fruit.

Fertility is always a primary concern because it ensures the future of the species. It was the custom at wedding parties to shower the bridal couple with seeds and fruits, a ritual that promised the blessing of children for the newlyweds. The importance of fertility is also suggested by the picture on an ancient Greek gemstone which depicts a winnowing device suspended above the images of Eros and Psyche, both veiled. This veiling — a custom that was always observed in the case of the bride — signifies a woman's consecration to mother earth and her ritual burial in the womb of the earth. Psyche's appearance on the gem, showered with grain, is an impressive sign that the strength of fertility is being transferred to her. The winnow that is spreading the grain over the couple is meant to produce good seed. Soon the parents will lay their child, the fruit of the seed, in the winnowing basket, thus renewing the cycle.

The cosmic connection between the human being and grain makes it clear that the symbolic equation of child and grain is balanced by the parallel equation of "corpse and grain." In fact, as far as grain is concerned, birth is best understood in the manner in which the ancients experienced everything — as components of the totality of being. Thus our origins are most intimately tied to death, and death is only another side of life — not its end! Both together are fundamentally the double-sided expression of what happens in nature: movement and countermovement, ascent and descent, inhaling and exhaling in the rhythmic conduct of being. The human corpse is delivered to the womb of the earth like a seed. For the pious pagan this meant that the dead were buried with the hope of a resurrection comparable to that of the seed and the grain.

It was also believed that the dead under the earth had the power to make the fruit come up from the earth, and for this reason one prayed to the spirits of the dead and the souls of the ancestors. Thus, in the sprouting ears of wheat which decorated a vase used to honor a grave in ancient Italy, one may see an image of the dead person buried there. In ancient Greece and elsewhere, it was a custom to sow seeds of grain on the new grave "so that for the dead person a cradle may be prepared like that of a mother."[2] In ancient India, there existed a similar custom. "To the roots of the plants the fathers are sliding," said the Brahmans. As the mother's womb of the earth transforms the dead seed into a new birth, so the rites and customs surrounding the burial of the dead assist the earth in bringing the dead to new life.

SYMBOL OF SALVATION

Rites of a similar kind are widespread. It is through them that the human being seeks to acquire the power of life that resides in the symbol of grain. Only through such rites can a person master the power of life and bestow it on those who are lacking it absolutely: the dead. This effort was supported by the treasured ritual food given the name *panspermy.* This mixture of cooked grains of wheat and the fruits of other seeds was served to the guests at funeral meals and then brought to the grave of the deceased. Rites of this kind require a genuine symbolic thinking, a knowledge of the essential relationship between the human person and grain.

Yet these rites also prove that a human being does not want to accept nature's inexorable cycle of death and birth with the placidity characteristic of plants. A person's spirit, a person's dignity rebel against the yoke of this cosmic necessity. That is the reason for the fervent longing for a redemption that permits a person to escape from the wheel of blind natural necessity. It is the basic religious disposition of the human being that seeks such a liberation. The fact that this desire for liberation was connected to the symbol of grain shows to what extent the fruit of the grain was an image of salvation pointing to the beyond.

It is true — the ancients searched for and saw the sacred in everything! And so they were awed by the numinous power they saw in grain, because it came to them from the hand of Demeter, a motherly deity who enjoyed the highest veneration. The sign of this divine earth mother can undoubtedly be recognized in the golden sheaf in the grave of Demeter. As on the grave, so the hand of the priestess may have clasped it often during her life when the mysteries of the ancient deities were celebrated and the power in grain and ear revealed itself as holy.

Most prominent among the sacred rituals in honor of the gods of ancient Greece were the Eleusinian mysteries, ceremonies which focused on the search for immortality and happiness in a future world. Eleusis, a small town near Athens, was known as "the place of salvation." In Eleusinian piety, nothing was as obvious as the reverence for the grain, the gift of Demeter, and the hope for a beatific life which was attached to this symbol.

This hope was the focal point of the cult of the divine grain mother Demeter and her daughter Persephone who, according to the cult's legend, was abducted by Pluto, the god of the underworld. Persephone eventually returned from the realm of the dead in order to save the world which was withering away because of Demeter's furious distress. The grain's power of salvation was revealed in the autumnal repetition of this redemptive event. Those who sought the favor of the gods — among them Sophocles, Plato, and Cicero — were seeking something incomparably higher than the hope for a naturally exalted life in this world and a cosmic rebirth to a new mortal existence. They sought an ultimate happy arrival at the goal of human life or, in the words of the Athenian orator Isocrates, they wanted nothing less than "the joyous hope for all of eternity."[3]

What was it that could awaken such an audacious confidence? Because of the extreme secrecy that surrounded cultic practices, only scant information has leaked out. Hippolytus of Rome testified that the "unspeakable" had been "the great and wonderful and perfect performance of the mysteries: a grain of wheat nourished in silence."[4] When the sacred celebration had reached its climax, a cut ear of wheat was displayed as representing salvation for time and eternity. With this sign the chief priest made the sacred appear in the temple which had been enveloped in the deep silence of the night—and into which a clear light suddenly fell. Innumerable ears of wheat exist in the world. From where did the power of this one come?

CULT OF THE HOLY GRAIN

That power is founded in the cult. Here, because of the required vow of silence, the unspeakable mystery of Eleusis converged on the ear of wheat. It was a mystery associated with the goddess Persephone. During the ritual celebrations, in the midst of the darkened temple, it was this goddess of the underworld whom the worshippers glimpsed, bathed in light, within the holy grain. When the celebration of the mystery reached its climax, something happened to the participant in the presence of the grain that saved them. Hippolytus named it "mystery."

The ritual was performed to make the "resurrection" of Persephone from the realm of the dead visibly present, thereby guaranteeing salvation in this world and the world to come to those who saw her. Whoever has seen this symbol of the coming goddess can depart in the blessed certitude of dying with great hope.[5] According to the Homeric hymn to Demeter, "among the people on earth the one who has seen this show is overjoyed. Whoever has not been initiated into the holy mysteries, whoever did not participate in them . . . walks along like 'a dead one in oppressive darkness'" (verse 481).

The highly regarded happiness of the Eleusinian mystics therefore has a metaphysical significance. The happiness was the result of participating in the celebration. This caused a difference between those who were initiated into the mysteries and those who were not. It was a separation here and now through which one group of people had become happy, while all others walk toward death unfulfilled and uncertain. The end of life thus assumes two faces. One glows with joy and gives to existence a special radiance. The other remains gloomy and applies to all *others:* an indeterminable crowd lacking any distinguishable characteristics.

The cultic celebrations in Eleusis shed light on the meaning of the many funeral rites that use the symbol of the grain of wheat. But they do more than that. They reflect the significance which this fascinating religious phenomenon had in relation to the Greek desire to achieve mastery over life itself. The Eleusinian mysteries were more than a common celebration, they included the whole world. According to the belief of these pious people, not only did the continuance of their own nation depend upon these mysteries, but they held together the whole human race. They were linked not only to the Athenian and Greek existence, but to the entire human existence.

One ancient writer, Vettius Agorius Praetextatus, explained that life *(bíos)* would be "unlivable" *(abíotos)* for the Greeks if these mysteries were no longer celebrated.[6] The ear of wheat that was displayed during the night of celebrating the Eleusinian mysteries was for Greek believers the holiest of symbols, the symbol on which the salvation of the world and the eternal life of the initiated depended.

Of course, the events linked with this cultic symbol were only a shadowy prefiguration of the true act of salvation. Yet the Advent-like expectation of salvation in Eleusis was truly a cry to heaven. We may rightly ask why the incarnate God—whose own "cultic mystery" would soon be established—would reveal to the Greeks in particular the sign of the grain of wheat, a sign that would inevitably touch their very hearts. Jesus had told them, "The hour has come for the Son of Man to be glorified. Very truly, unless a grain of wheat falls into the earth and dies, it remains only a single grain; but if it dies, it bears much fruit" (John 12:23–24).

The question prods us to consider first the purpose of such images. These words were spoken by Jesus at the time of his triumphal entry into Jerusalem, one of the most profound moments in the gospel of John. With the gloom of his approaching passion already closing in on him, the Lord uses the image of the grain of wheat to announce his life-giving dying. Is it too daring to believe that the symbol of the dying seed — a symbol that is as great as it is mean — exists only because the Son of God wanted from all eternity to go to his death as the Son of Man? Dare we believe that the germination and budding of the seed happen only because the crucified God rose from the dead?

It was he who brought the world the new birth that rescued the earth from its natural transience and for which the human soul had so long desired. "No being can exist except by means of an image of God's perfection" (Claudel). The grain and ear of wheat, too, exist ultimately only as the image of God's perfection which appeared in Christ. They are images that depict something of Christ and his incomparable mystery of creating and rescuing the world. They announce the redemption of the world, a redemption that was the fruit of him who brought salvation by sacrificing himself.

THE PRIMORDIAL GRAIN

It is therefore no accident that Jesus addressed those profoundly meaningful words about the dying and fruit-bearing grain of wheat to the Greeks who had come to Jerusalem for the Passover. The Greeks in particular had to be receptive to the parable of the grain of wheat because they knew of Eleusis and its mysterious rituals which reached their climax in the sign of the ear of wheat. They come upon Jesus, and he meets their desire with this discreet gesture which revealed to their inner eye an image, a symbol of salvation with which they were especially familiar.

He revealed himself, with restraint but also with emphasis, as the holy grain, the first grain, the primordial grain[7] that had been anticipated with a deep and ancient yearning. He came into the world in order to lead humanity to the eternally salvific exaltation of his glorified person, an exaltation into which his still solitary humanity would soon be transformed through the cross and grave. Some day humanity would see him in the glory he had had in the Father's presence before the world existed (John 17:5). Truly he was "the spiritual grain that fell on a single spot and rose bearing fruit throughout the world."[8]

Yet from a symbolic perspective Jesus' words of revelation to the Greeks has a significance for the history of the world that goes far beyond the borders of Hellenism. After all, they are the answer to an impenetrable question which permeated the whole pagan world. The ancients did have a general understanding — a primordial but unexplained tradition — that the gift of the field comes from the *sacrifice.* The significance of both plant and human fertility could not be derived simply by considering these events in isolation; they had to be set in motion again and again. For this to happen, blood had to flow, and what was alive had to die. The primitive people lived with the never-ending anxiety that the useful powers of the world — the sun, the moon, and the germinating potential of the soil — could at some time exhaust themselves. That anxiety became stronger in those periods when the life forces of nature seemed to expire.

Such fears tormented the ancients most acutely when they suspected that they themselves were responsible for the depletion of those powers because they had gathered the first fruits of the season and harvested the ripe crop, thus plundering the forces of growth. That is why the first fruits of vegetative and animal life are sacrificed — to placate the mysterious forces and ensure that their bounty may be used without danger. Rites of this kind often mark the beginning of a new year. In many cultures they take place in spring, the period of cosmic renewal. It was once a widespread custom to sow grain at the time of the spring equinox. Even today the descendants of the Tartars scatter seed into a pitcher filled with earth in remembrance of the creation.

One cannot help but realize how symbolic it is that Christians in the northern hemisphere celebrate the feast of the resurrection in spring, at a time when the world's greatest traditions celebrated the beginning of a new year. Precisely when nature was in the process of renewing itself, the hope of Christianity expected the universal resurrection of all flesh. So too was the biblical Passover celebrated in the spring. Thus it is significant that Jesus spoke of the dying and rising grain of wheat during this season. Who doesn't sense the underlying connections?

The primordial instinct of people to maintain their own being and the existence of the world by securing vegetative, animal, and human fertility was probably the basis of all human sacrifice. Gradually animal sacrifices, primarily the sacrifice of bulls, replaced their human counterparts. The connection between sacrifice and re-birth becomes clear in the Persian myth of Mithras, the god of the sun. When Mithras slays a bull, wheat sprouts out of its spine and grape vines grow out of its blood. On the marble display which portrays this myth in the British Museum, Mithras' dagger is still in the wound, and instead of blood, three full ears of wheat are emerging from it. Elsewhere the tail of the bull ends in sheaves of wheat.

Investigations into these connections reveal a tremendous internal struggle with regard to the frightful sacrifices of human beings which were offered at harvest time for the success of the harvest. One could consider them correctly as "sacrifices of regeneration"; seen in this way, they had the meaning of a ritual repetition of creation. In fact, a widely-found tradition says that the world originated from the violent death of a divine being. It was believed that herbs, plants and fruits of the field, the grain of wheat, and grapevines grew out of the flesh and blood of the dismembered victim. In ancient Egypt the Osiris religion also understood wheat in this sense. There one made reproductions of the murdered god of vegetation using mud from the Nile and filled them with grains of wheat. In the sprouting of the grains was seen the revival of the god and, with him, the renewal of nature.

Here, as in similar cults, people sought to understand the paradox that was so central to their existence: the fertility on which they depend is a gift from the hand of death. Dying, being sacrificed, is the prerequisite for the growth of wheat and any other fruit. Therefore the sacrifice of a human being at harvest time—that is, for the renewal of the power of nature that reveals itself in the harvest—was no less than a symbolic repetition of the act of creation, an act in which the life of a god was sacrificed for the fertility of the grain.

Such myths and rites, as one increasingly recognizes today, are instructive not only for the elementary questions concerning the historical events at Eleusis. They disclose, in fact, the depths of the symbolism of the grain of wheat and offer a deeper understanding of the Lord's use of this image. In view of his own death and resurrection the incarnate Son, with divine authority, appropriated to himself the holy symbol which many ancient religions had venerated as a gift and manifestation of a dying and rising deity. "Anyone who sows corn sows holiness," says ancient Persian wisdom. Yet this wisdom tradition was unable to envision precisely which "holy sign" and which "salvation" the human race was sowing with each grain of wheat into the waiting earth.

MODEL OF CHRIST'S PASSION

Grain also played a significant role — and this reveals the religious background of the symbol — as an image of suffering. "Who can describe the wheat's suffering when it is being crushed? How many torments does it have to bear?" asks Ephraem the Syrian. "It is being tortured in order to provide its torturers with their livelihood."[9] Remember that Ephraem once said that the key to the richness of this symbol is the passion and death — and ultimate resurrection — of the Lord. This is what the Syrian poet Cyrillona meant when he declared that the creator constructed the model of his passion in the wheat. He amplifies this analogy as follows:

> The wheat remains silent when it is crushed, as did the Lord when he was condemned to death. It does not cry out when it is killed; nor did our Lord when he was crucified. It surrenders itself to the hand which kills it, as our Lord surrendered himself to his captors [was "Jews"]. It leaves behind its husks, as our Lord left behind the linen wrappings when he rose from the grave. The wheat, crushed in silence, becomes a corpse, then comes to life again while it is hidden. Outwardly it appears as if it had died miserably, but in reality it lives and grows abundantly. . . . It carries its children: its daughters, the ears of wheat, climb on its shoulders. They rise above its head.[10]

For those who understand the unspoken language of creation, how eloquently do the silent signs of nature speak, especially in their "passion," in the meaning of suffering! Christ, the grain of wheat, did in fact rise and unravel this secret language. He removed the meaninglessness from the world's suffering because, as the Christ-grain, he brought final resurrection for all who apprehend the grace of his ascension and thus the meaning of their own suffering. The worldly grain of wheat is a sign of the paschal turning point for the world and for life. "We saw it buried naked," says Ephraem, "and we saw it rise in glory. It was a silent corpse which began to stir in the dust. . . . Incomprehensible is its nakedness which was swallowed up by glory."[11]

Indeed, it is an incomprehensible and yet utterly simple image which reflects the terrible—and from the merely human point of view, nonsensical—decision of God to give, through his death, life to the world and participation in his glory! Did those Greeks who came to Jerusalem to celebrate the Passover possibly understand the significance of the Lord's words? Scripture says nothing about it. The Messiah could reveal the profound meaning of this parable only by allowing it to happen in reality and through the blood of his own humanity. But ultimately it would be revealed only to those who would embrace with him the human destiny of the grain of wheat. Only when God and humanity join in the passion and resurrection which Christ made accessible to all does the connection between death and fruit become true. Only then can it actually touch humanity to a degree that is beyond any imagination. "The fruit of Christ's passion is the life of all, of the dead as well as of the living. Because the death of Christ became the seed of life."[12]

In fact, the grain and ear of wheat were created precisely in order to point toward this world-redeeming event. It is their eternal honor to be an image of the salvation of all people through the death and resurrection of Christ. The evangelist John reported the historical reality when he wrote about the grain of wheat. This reality becomes present sacramentally in the mysteries of the church. In fact, it is imprinted as the fundamental law of the life and death of every Christian. The true redeemer fully reveals this long-foreknown meaning of grain and ear. After Eleusis had for so long offered a sight of the holy fruit of the grain in a blind foreshadowing, the eternal Word revealed himself with human lips as its primordial reality.

The early church revered this symbol because of its power. It was, after all, in both word and image, the sign of that bread-breaking and wine-spilling on the cross in which the church was permitted to participate and at which she was always present as witness and hidden collaborator. Moved by an old picture of the descent from the cross, a contemporary poet brings the connection immediately to life:

> Grain of wheat,
> not produced by earthly means,
> fall out of the golden background!
> Break, break into the table!
> Bent naked over the shroud,
> you break the bread in the middle,
> pour the wine.[13]

For the early Christians the intimate relationship between the fruit of the grain and sacramental nourishment was so obvious that they pictured the eucharist through the symbol of the ear of wheat. As the colorful pictures on the graves of the catacombs show, Christians decorated the places of their liturgical celebration with scenes of the wheat harvest. During the eucharistic meal they intoned the harvest songs from the psalms which we still sing today. Even now the ears of wheat remain a popular symbolic decoration for liturgical vessels and vestments. Moreover, the verse of the psalm about the feeding of the people of God with the finest wheat (Psalm 81:16) remains for the church a liturgical song of gratitude for the bread of the Lord's table.

Perhaps one could object that we are only playing around with an image that could just as well be replaced with the image of the bread itself. But that would not be correct. Wherever in the sphere of liturgy or ecclesiastical art the symbol of the ear or grain of wheat has been chosen in order to represent the eucharistic bread, these signs point to a unique and urgent dimension of this mystery; namely, that by tasting this bread Christians "proclaim the Lord's death until he comes" (1 Corinthians 11:26). The sign of this death is, as our Lord himself attested, the fruit of the grain. The bread is a symbol because of its essence as food. But the ear of wheat symbolizes the fruit of the grain that had died. Thus the ear of wheat can point in a language entirely its own to the hidden meaning of the eucharistic bread: the dying of the Christ-grain.

Seen in this light, the symbolic power of both the grain and ear are integral to the symbolism of bread, just as the wheat is indispensable for the miracle of the sacrament. Without the wheat "the altars would stand bare and the Holy Spirit could not descend; without it the sacrament of atonement would not take place; without it, indeed, no human being would be capable of appeasing the deity," said Cyrillona. In the eucharist "the forgiveness of sins emanates from the bread," just as it does from the gaping side of the Savior which, in its visible appearance, is reminiscent of the ear of wheat: "split, torn open and yet closed in on itself" just as it exists in nature.[14] At the table of the Lord the salvific power of the primordial grain of wheat permeates not only the human soul but also the human body. It continues that transformation which will be completed with the renewal of all things at the end of time (Matthew 19:28).

Irenaeus wholeheartedly contends that the joyful hope of the early Christians in the resurrection had its origin in the primordial grain of wheat that became the eucharistic bread. He writes:

> We know that the grain of wheat, after it has fallen into the earth and there disintegrates, reappears through the power of God's all-encompassing Spirit in manifold ways. In God's wisdom the fruit of the vine and the wheat subsequently serve God's people for when the divine word transforms the elements of bread and wine, they become the body and blood of Christ. So too our bodies, nourished by the eucharist, will be lowered into the earth and, after they have disintegrated, will rise again when their time has come. The word of the Lord will give them the resurrection in the glory of the Father who endows that which is mortal with immortality, and that which is perishable with imperishability.[15]

"LIFE-GIVING GRAIN OF WHEAT"

If one considers the hope of immortality which the believers of ancient religions attached to the symbol of the grain of wheat and the nourishment it suggests, then the connection between the eucharist and eschatological rebirth, seen here so clearly, is readily embraced as the noble completion of grand expectations. Thus we discover the basis of the Christian joy of being. Early Christianity anchored its hope for the resurrection of the flesh on the power of the eucharist as the true "life-giving grain of seed."[16]

The words of Irenaeus are clear about this. They give liturgical meaning to the parable of the seed of wheat that Paul wove into his First Letter to the Corinthians. This too was certainly no accident. Undoubtedly most of those who became Christians in the earliest Corinthian community had been members of groups which cultivated the pagan mysteries. The image of the ear of wheat would have been very familiar to them, just as the Greeks who were in Jerusalem for the Passover would have grasped the significance of the Lord's words about the grain of wheat. Paul writes:

> But someone will ask, "How are the dead raised? With what kind of body do they come?" Fool! What you sow does not come to life until it dies. And as for what you sow, you do not sow the body that is to be, but a bare seed, perhaps of wheat or of some other grain. . . . So it is with the resurrection of the dead. What is sown is perishable, what is raised is imperishable. It is sown in dishonor, it is raised in glory. It is sown in weakness, it is raised in power. It is sown a physical body, it is raised a spiritual body (1 Corinthians 15:35 – 44).

Paul leaves no doubt that the human being is also subjected to the law of the dying and rising seed of grain. Irenaeus elucidates the passage this way: According to this law, the same thing happens to humanity that happened to Jesus. The grain of the carnal body of Jesus becomes in the eucharist the sacramental body, thus enabling the human being to be conformed mystically but really to the grain which is Christ. Through the eucharistic food Christians themselves turn into the Christ-grain so that when their earthly body perishes, the power of the eucharistic meal will transform them totally into the glory of the resurrection. Thus their bitter dying—whether it be the darkness of a quick death or a slow fading away—becomes for them a crossing over with Christ: the dawning of a new life whose seeds are resting already now in the faithful through the bread of immortality. Here the profound parallel between humanity and the grain of wheat, which had been intimated in ancient cultic practices, becomes concrete and is fulfilled beyond measure.

John of Damascus expands on the Pauline meditation: "Therefore consider the seeds buried in the furrows and in the graves. Who is it that gives them roots, reeds, leaves, ears, and the finest blades? Is it not the creator of all things? Is it not God's command that gives them life? Therefore believe that in like manner the resurrection of the dead will happen through God's beck and call."[17]

We hear again from the Syrian poet Cyrillona: "The wheat repulses its decay, shoots up, and returns to life in itself and out of itself. Likewise, our own body will be renewed after its destruction and will continue to exist for all eternity."[18] It is the ancient symbolism of the grain of wheat, confirmed by the incarnate Son and his apostle, which finds expression in the following verses of the poet Prudentius. In a hymn for the occasion of a burial he writes:

Sic semina sicca virescunt
iam mortua iamque sepulta,
quae reddita caespite ab imo
veteres meditantur aristas.

The dry seeds—dead,
buried in the field—
already they sprout anew
from the depth,
become green
and train themselves to carry ears.[19]

These ancient ideas still echo in Schiller's *The Song of the Bell:*

To holy earth's dark, silent bosom
We our handiwork resign,
The husbandmen the seed consign

And bless the sower, by laws divine.
Still costlier seed, in sorrow bringing,
We hide within the lap of earth,
And hope that, from the coffin springing,
'Twill bloom in brighter beauty forth.[20]

Everlasting harvest, birth without death — this is the promise seen in the grain of wheat that symbolizes Christ. And it is seen here and now. Growing unceasingly, out of the primordial grain is the fruit of the people of God.[21] With the eyes of faith we see the "holy grains of wheat"[22] ripen into an imponderably rich harvest. Because the grain of wheat — that is, Jesus — let itself be buried, it did not remain alone. It is risen, but not in its former solitude. Its dying-and-rising is the mystery of the death and resurrection of the real and perfect body of Christ, the church;[23] it is the redemption of all peoples. The grain that was not generated by earthly means surrendered itself to let sprout the salvation of all.[24] Miraculously multiplied by the fruit of its destruction, the primordial grain of wheat, with its daughters and their load of new seed, arose from that grave in the springtime garden.

And thus is the paschal mystery wondrously revealed in the ear of wheat. Cyrillona writes:

> This glorious fortress, this ear that has risen out of itself! The wheat sprouts up out of the midst of all of its opponents and looks down from the height as did . . . our Lord when he had risen from the grave. Its cruciform stem carries the weight so that it does not fall down. . . . Thrown into the earth it died. But that which had died was awakened. And that which was buried alone appears again in the company of its companions. It is surrounded and embraced by its children, neighbors, siblings, and friends. Thus the ear of wheat forms the model of the resurrection and proclaims to those who see it: As I who was buried came to life again, in the same way the dead who are resting in the dust will also live again.[25]

Yet another dimension of the paschal mystery is revealed in the symbol of the ear of wheat. It is the symbol's profoundly *feminine* aspect, as, according to Ephraem the Syrian, the buried grain rises from the soil like a crowned bride.[26] Cyrillona sees it coming up "like a mother with her daughters."[27] Perhaps an echo of the power of the symbol in the history of religion resonates in these images. The true and pure reality of God which they reflect refers to humanity only in relationship to Christ. Only through Christ's death did God become our mother — this hidden maternity emerged visibly, in the birth of the church, from the torn heart of the Son. How beautifully did the Syrian church leaders suggest this meaning! Based on its use in the cults of the Greek and oriental mysteries, it is not difficult to see how literally one has to understand the comparison they used.

But as Christians we also know the sacred temple or house of consecration in which the ancient image becomes reality: the tent of the new people of God. Unceasingly, on the altar of Christ's sacrifice occurs a "holy marriage" which gives birth to Christians out of the death and resurrection of the savior.

Here in the house of consecration of the grain mother — that is, the church — the ancient equation of humanity and grain constantly finds its fulfillment. In the mystery of the Christian liturgy the believer is conformed to the primordial grain and its fate, dying and rising with it. Life out of death — indeed, life *in* death — is the law of the grain's being. It stands as the overarching emblem of Christian existence because it is the law of the mystery of Christ. Whether mystically (in the sacrifice of the altar) or practically (in everything our daily routine happens to include), the Christian experiences both the heights and the depths of what it means to be sacramentally adapted to Christ-the-wheat. "Look! From the one body of Christ — what a harvest of martyrs grew out of it!"[28] In whatever form, whether bloody or bloodless, the Christian becomes a witness through the power of the eucharistic food, food which itself bears witness to the possibility of life from death. It is precisely in this lived identification with the Lord that Christians find a foretaste of that which is prepared for them in the sign of the grain's destiny: life in the eternal harvest festival.

This final destination is illuminated for us by the harvest pictures in the catacombs in which reapers and cherubic infants mow the ripened grain. These pictures illustrated for the early Christians the destiny prepared for them after the harvest time of persecution — refuge in the eternal barns and the harvest feast of the "divine farmer whose . . . barn contains all mysteries."[29]

The poet Werner Bergengruen envisions the mystery this way:

You called on us early. Yet we comprehended late.
Your field is the world. We are sown as your grain. . . .
The field is many things. The grain did not choose,
yet it contained a yearning when it was scattered.
Whether it fell into a thicket of thorns,
on solid granite, on fertile soil or arid sand,
the place is predetermined.
Wait, grain, for time! Put forth your buds.
What happens is not your decision.
Entrust yourself to the swing of the sower's hand:
where you fall, there is your proper field.
About every grain it is also said
that it must die in order to produce fruit.
So, grain, give yourself to death.
You will not remain alone in darkness.
The command of him who sowed you will be your escort.
His field is the world. We are sown as his grain.
He called on us early. Yet we comprehended late.
Already the evening light is growing.
The mist clears up,
and beyond this world,
something else reveals itself.[30]

Here the symbolism of grain speaks to present experience. Especially during times of crisis — and this poem was written during the Nazi persecutions — the voices of the martyrs soon proved how the symbol of grain helped humanity see through its destiny and to accept it lovingly. Tertullian's famous saying calls the blood of the martyrs the "seed of Christians."[31] Saint Agatha was granted a vision of her impending martyrdom which used the image of a threshing. Just as the thresher smashes the ears of wheat to pieces, so will the sufferings of persecution smash the mortal frame of human beings so that the ripe grain may be liberated for heaven.[32]

Similarly, the aged martyr and bishop Ignatius of Antioch saw his martyrdom in the sign of the grain's fate. On his journey to Rome, where the beasts of prey were waiting for him in the coliseum, his ardent longing to be identified with the Christ-grain makes him call out: "I am the wheat of Christ; I want to be crushed by the teeth of the beasts so that I will be found to be pure bread."[33]

These examples should make one thing clear: Absolute acceptance of this symbol—with all that it implies—is for the Christian a matter of faith; indeed, it is a measure of the degree of his or her faith. When such faith confronts the challenges of Christian living, the holy images conjured up by the following acclamation are never "outdated."

> O grain of wheat,
> you—our last hope,
> you—our refuge in need![34]

PART TWO

BREAD

THE SEED DIES

Once the lovely grain of wheat has born fruit, a significant portion of the grain must be returned to the earth as seed. But the far greater portion of the wheat becomes bread, and thus, as food, is transformed into a higher life, a human life — thereby achieving its natural completion. Wheat grows into food, a staple source of life. From transformation to transformation the grain evolves until it becomes the "beloved bread," a primary source of human nourishment.

This connection is reflected in the use of the word "loaf" for bread; "loaf" has its etymological root in the word "live." There are several common expressions which clearly indicate the extent to which bread is the embodiment of the human life and livelihood. We speak, for example, of the "bread-winner" or of "casting one's bread upon the waters," in the sense of acting charitably with no thought of personal gain. A person needs to "know on which side one's bread is buttered" while the phrase "bread and butter" refers to a sense of elementary considerations. Finally, "to take the bread out of one's mouth" means to deprive someone of his or her livelihood.

In order to become this bread, the grain of wheat must perish and rise again. The destiny of the "primordial grain," Jesus, was in no way different. It fell into the soil and came out of it transformed in order to become "the bread from heaven that gives life to the world" (John 6:33).

From where this bread came to us
which removed from us every need —
we will here tell the story.
The seed was first sown by him
who created and formed all things

since he has power over everything.
This is the wise farmer . . .
it is the paternal God.
When he saw the world in its distress,
then his seed was sent down
to this desolate land
with the power of the Holy Spirit
from whom a maid corporally
and truly humanly conceived a child.[35]

OUR DAILY BREAD

Indeed, to become bread for us, the Son of the Father was sown by the Holy Spirit into the Virgin Mary's womb. After being slain by the hatred of unbelief, he entered into the womb of the grave. It was out of merciful love for humanity that Jesus desired to live the image of the grain of wheat from beginning to end.

When he, promised offspring of the woman, was finally born, the birth took place in Bethlehem, the town whose name means "house of bread." God comes and lies as a whimpering child in a manger in order to be able to invigorate all the faithful with the wheat of his body.[36] How meaningful therefore are the medieval portraits which show Mary in a vestment made of ears of wheat, or poetic references to Mary as a gift of wheat. Significant too are pictures of the divine child lying on ears of wheat in the manger. Even the liturgy testifies to the power of the symbols when, at the feast of the Annunciation, the Orthodox church addresses the one who bore God with the words: "As an unploughed field you let sprout the divine ear of wheat!"

All of this confirms that the promised savior—already at the time of his incarnation—was oriented toward "becoming bread." The heavenly grain of wheat fell into the earth to become bread for a famished world. The very life of God became human, became bread.

Bread is life. In fact, it is the symbol of every food that nourishes the human being. No one knows this better than the person who is hungry.

Bread is the simple name for the most basic need of our bodies, and no one has a better understanding of this need than God, our creator. Did not God's incarnate Son himself teach us this in the Lord's Prayer when he placed the petition, "Give us this day our daily bread" first among those focused on human needs?

Of course, this prayer which is so closely tied to our human, earthly condition does not simply tell us to ask our heavenly Father to still the hunger of our body and care for our vital necessities. Who else but the Son of Man understood the significance of bread in God's saving plan? Who else saw as he did its dignity as a sign, an image of the triune abundance of life we so deeply desire?

We can surmise that the Lord was aware of the life-giving potential of bread, not only when he taught his disciples the Lord's Prayer, but whenever he broke and shared bread. The Fathers of the church consistently suggest this understanding when they show their preference for interpreting the prayer's plea for bread eucharistically. How could Christians ever again completely satisfy their earthly hunger by bread alone once the gift of finest wheat had become their holiest symbol, a symbol in which the eternal Word of God is joined with perishable nourishment?

And yet a casual — and therefore the truly inhuman — attitude in regard to bread remains a common human temptation. It is a temptation that the children of Adam and Eve have inherited from generation to generation, ever since they gave in to the temptation by wrongful eating. But precisely for this reason is it so significant that the redeemer begins his public life by exemplifying the proper attitude toward bread when he was tempted in the desert. That encounter exemplifies the on-going tension between the temporal and eternal nourishment that bread provides and the parallel correspondence between these two aspects of human nature. Jesus explicitly exemplifies his attitude toward bread when he freely permits himself to experience a very real physical hunger for this food. Thus would he come to know the torture of a body screaming for bread, a torture which his ancestors wandering in the desert had also known.

For Jesus the first test of his vocation was perhaps the most cruel of the satanic challenges. Confronting a man who after forty days of fasting was bodily exhausted and in whom the natural need for food finally and irresistibly demanded its right, the tempter depicts for Jesus' starving senses the color and form, the aroma and taste of a fresh loaf of bread. "Hungry? Bread! Here is bread, as much as you want, as soon as you really want it. If you truly are the Son of God, than you have only to command that these stones become bread. Say it!"

Despite his agony, Jesus resists the overpowering temptation to perform a miracle just this once for his own benefit. The Son of God opposes this irresistible, mouth-watering enticement of the edible bread: "It is written, 'One does not live by bread alone but by every word that comes from the mouth of God'" (Matthew 4:4). With his sole weapon a verse from the Book of Deuteronomy (8:3), the starving victor beats the tempting enemy and in so doing reveals the ancient biblical event of bread in the desert to be a prefiguring sign of his own life-giving bread.

BREAD OF LIFE

The test to which the Messiah subjected himself in his first conflict with Satan is the basic human peril since Adam's fall; it is the primordial temptation to live "by bread alone," thereby forgetting that bread and all other foods are only a sign for the life that comes from the mouth of God. By overcoming his temptation, the savior abruptly pulls humanity out of the life-threatening danger of a craving for bread that is contrary to God's will. For humanity, created in God's image, bread alone is never sufficient. Bread, no matter how savory its aroma and how hearty its taste, is the preeminent sign of a higher "bread of life" which comes forth as Word from the mouth of God.

Bread of God, Word of God! Certainly, God's Word, too, is bread, something edible that people may devour it like the prophet did with the sealed scroll (see Ezekiel 2:1 — 3:4). It is something they shall consume completely like bread, with mouth and teeth and the tasting tongue. Bread and Word! Jesus, who at the beginning of his work of salvation revealed the God-given bond between the two images, is himself the Word and the bread of life. He is God's Word in person, the incarnate Word of the Father. Thus it is a deeply meaningful sign that the entire public life and work of Jesus takes place between these two scenes: his temptation with bread in the desert and his breaking of the bread during the last supper. Only he who withstood the temptation of the bread could become the guardian of bread for the deadly hunger of the earth. Only he could be the bread of life.

However, in between the two events which mark the beginning and end of his public life, Jesus makes a eucharistic announcement at Capernaum. There he declares, to the annoyance of purely human reasoning, that he himself is the bread of life which came down from heaven. The crowd, which would have been spontaneously reminded of the miracle of manna in the desert by Jesus' multiplication of the loaves, presses forward toward Jesus. But they do so — and his restrained rebuke makes this clear — only out of curiosity and for the pure pleasure of eating because they had already been filled. He rebukes them for seeking only earthly bread. He has been sent to nourish them with better food, to prepare them for the only bread that fully satisfies and stills all human hungers.

Because they ask Jesus for a miracle like that of the manna in the desert so that they may believe in him, he reveals himself to them, shockingly enough, as the bread come down from heaven, the greatest miracle "*I am* the bread of life. . . . The bread that I will give for the life of the world is my flesh" (John 6:48 – 51).

It is I, the great question of the world, the bread of incomprehensible astonishment. Indeed, I am the bread of opposition, of the unheard-of divine challenge. "This teaching is difficult; who can accept it?" (John 6:60) *I am bread* — truly, really. Those who hear him demand an explanation, yet he gives none. He insists on his emphatically spoken word; he demands the most unbelievable faith. His only proof, his almost incomprehensible concession: He shows them a reality that corresponds to the image.

Through the incarnate Word, God's mouth expressed his thought about bread clearly and audibly. Jesus dares to tell the resistant crowd what bread means to him, what bread should tell about him. He declares that all bread ought to be a distinct Word, a transparent image of an unimaginable deed of God present in the Son. In order to make the image contained in bread completely visible, the Word became bread, bread on the table of an earthly meal.

Foolish wisdom of God's love: The same bread that nourishes our body shall become divine food for us—God's "flesh for the life of the world." On the evening before his passion the Lord kept the shocking promise he had made at Capernaum. *The word became bread* during the ritual of the Last Supper when the Son of Man instituted his highest mystery and completed that "union" of word and bread that he had initiated at the beginning of his public life in opposition to his Satanic tempter. "As often as you do this" becomes, from this moment on, the basis of the ritual as it was initiated by the Lord. The earthly bread becomes the Word, and the Word becomes bread.

BREAD: A WORD OF DOUBLE SIGNIFICANCE

This action at the last supper is the total reversal and the redemptive redress of that disastrous meal in the garden at the beginning of humanity's history. Now that fatal eating is set against the meal that gives life, and the food that was the means of the break with God is supplanted by the food which forges a new and eternal bond with God. The companionship of creator and creature at table that God had desired from the very beginning is reestablished. The food, the eating is no longer a sign of disaster; it has become instead a sign of salvation. Had not Adam sinned, this table fellowship would have always been the sign of God's highest intention for us. Notice how much talk there is about eating and food in the first chapters of Genesis. God's first commandment, actually God's very first conversation with Adam, deals with food, the enjoyment of which would soon become a disaster for humanity's first parents and all their descendants.

Consequently the fate of the world depends, in one way or another, on eating, the rightness or wrongness of which signifies acceptance or abuse of God's intention for the food and the act of eating. After all, the food taken from the earth is, in its origin, symbolic of the divine vitality surrendering itself to the creature. The plants growing out of the earth, the herbs, and the trees are organs, God's fingertips, so-to-speak. In them God touches the world and keeps alive that which is living. Only in this way does one understands why eating which is in opposition to the living Word from God's mouth could become the means of a world catastrophe of such vast dimensions.

But does anyone still understand food and the act of eating as symbols? And yet, from beginning to end, Scripture insists that "bread" is a word of double significance and twofold value. It symbolizes two kinds of human nourishment, one sensual and the other beyond the sensual. Eating, it is true, is a physical process, but one in which God is intimately involved. By means of our bodily senses and organs, the art of eating is intended to nourish both our physical and spiritual hungers. We no longer remember God's role in giving us our daily bread; no longer do we realize that because of the last supper all bread has become so venerable that a Russian proverb is able to say: "When one puts bread on the table, the table becomes an altar."

Every crumb of bread reminds us of the redeemed earth's secret. Already at the sentencing of Adam and Eve in the garden, God makes mention of the daily bread; thus it becomes a meager yet merciful sign of the struggle between God and humanity for salvation and reconciliation. The savior and the bread—from the beginning they belong together. And until the end of time, bread, as a sign of God, challenges humanity to leave behind the perishable table at which they enjoy themselves in the shade of the tree of knowledge. Instead, at the Lord's supper they are to eat their way out of the foreign land into which their wrongful eating had led them. They are to eat their way out, just as the children of Israel hurriedly ate their way out of the misery of Egypt at that first Passover meal on the night of their exodus.

PAGAN ANALOGIES OF THE EUCHARIST

In light of the powerful role food and eating have played since the beginning of time, we must ask, "Were not the manifold cultic sacrificial meals that developed throughout the world simply the attempt of fallen humanity to reestablish its lost communion with God through the act of eating?" The belief that humans could unite themselves with a god by eating all or part of that god became increasingly more common. Just as primitive peoples were convinced that they could incorporate the strength of an animal or the superior capabilities of another person by eating their flesh, they also believed that they could share in divine power and vitality by eating something that is divine.

One is reminded of the cultic sacrifice of the Mexican Aztecs who on the feast of their main god, Huitzilópochtli, made a grandiose picture of the god from the dough of cake which they had prepared from the grains of wheat. They venerated the image with incense, sacrificial foods, and a solemn procession. Then, after shooting arrows at it, they declared it to be dead. The chief priest cut the heart out of the dead god and gave it to the king to eat. The subordinate priests broke the rest of the body into pieces and distributed them among the citizens as food. This rite was called *teocualo* — good food — and the ones fed with the holy bread "god's guardians."

Through this cultic meal the vitality of the god had thus transmitted itself, the celebrating crowd was convinced, to the god's followers, and therefore they believed themselves to be filled with god and sanctified through divine nourishment. The revulsion of the Spanish monks who considered such rites to be diabolic imitations of the Christian celebration of the eucharist does not astonish us.

Such a cultic sacrificial meal still intimates the ancient abomination of human sacrifice, though in its mitigated form it is simply an attempt to recreate the bloody sacrifice in the form of dough. Elsewhere, in both the Zoroastrian religion and in the cult of Mithras we encounter a liturgical celebration with bread and water (or perhaps bread and wine or a mixture with the haoma juice) — a celebration which included communion using the sacrificial food. Already the early Christian apologists argued against this cult because of its obviously striking analogy with the Christian sacrificial meal.[37]

The participants in the Eleusinian mysteries drank the Kykeon, a form of bread made into a drink consisting of flour, water, and spices. In this barley drink, too, people believed they received the saving gift of divine life, not only for their own redemption but also as pledge of union with the god. This union was open to the entire world. Initiation into these mysteries always renewed the ability of human beings to guard the cosmos against being overwhelmed by chaos.

These analogies show that, when at his last meal on earth our Lord inaugurated the eucharist, he obviously went back to an ancient cultic pair of symbols, the bread and wine, precisely because of their significance. His cult-establishing act comprised and redeemed the world; it also gave the symbols their most comprehensive meaning. In fact, in the very hour when he was about to abolish once and for all the ritual sacrifice of animals – actually, all bloody sacrifices — he reverts to bread and drink as an even older form of sacrifice. Thus he recalled the sacrificial meal which had been performed in its purest form in that magnificent liturgy offered by Melchizedek and Abraham in the royal palace before the Most High. The offering of the mysterious king of justice, who seems to appear both timeless and parentless out of the darkness of history only for this single priestly act, is recalled at the hour of the evening meal in the upper room, and since then at every new celebration of the eucharistic evening meal.

REDEMPTION OF PAGAN "SELF-SACRIFICES"

One thing is certain regarding all of these various prefigurations of a ritual divine meal, namely that a *sacrifice* was a prerequisite for the meal. The profound parallel with the Christian liturgical meal is clearly stated by Paul:

> Consider the people of Israel; are not those who eat the sacrifices partners in the altar? What do I imply then? That food sacrificed to idols is anything, or that an idol is anything? No, I imply what pagans sacrifice, they sacrifice to demons and not to God. I do not want you to be partners with demons. You cannot drink the cup of the Lord and the cup of demons. You cannot partake of the table of the Lord *and* the table of demons." (1 Corinthians 10:18 – 21)

As unique and incomparable the mystery of the Christian liturgy may be in its content — indeed, it is stunningly new — in its forms it nevertheless reaches back into time immemorial. Otherwise, how could it have been understood by human beings on this earth? And yet, precisely because of the claim that the true God brings to bear on humanity, a clear dividing line must now be drawn between the foreshadowings and the final form.

The communion with God into which humanity enters in the sacrificial meal does not tolerate communion with demons. For our purposes the Pauline statement above emphasizes that eating a sacrificial meal effects communion with the god to whom the altar is dedicated. Basically this statement is valid for the sacrificial rite of the Israelites as well as for the pagan cults. The reference to these rites would be impossible to understand or completely senseless if the pagan sacrificial meal had not already contained some hidden element of truth. In the pagan veneration of idols a remnant of genuine divine service was still alive.

Yet at the moment of the Lord's crucifixion, the self-sacrifices of the primordial divine beings which had been imagined in the various myths are redeemed and thereby dissolved in the truth of history and reality. Likewise, since that meal at which the Lord established the new covenant, the many-faceted ancient ritual of sacramentally-received sacrificial meals is once and for all annulled. The holy bread and the holy drink of the eucharist are now the only food of true *communio* between God and humanity because of the bloody self-sacrifice of the incarnate Son on the cross. The "nourishment of life attached to the cross"[38] — and the bread promised at Capernaum is certainly this: God's flesh for the life of the world! The bread of the altar is "food of the cross," "fruit of the sacrifice," as Odo Casel describes it. Truly, Christian eucharistic worship is the most awesome rite of sacrifice and meal. It is performed, however, in the most human style by means of these noble symbols of human culture.

TURNING PREMONITION INTO REALITY

From generation to generation these sacrificial rites pass on the shocking premonition, and often with primitive sensuality, that the death of a god is required in order that human beings may live. God waited until the time had come to let this premonition become historical reality. Then he turned into perfect reality what had been prefigured in ancient rites in so many ways —

not only in the sphere of the religion but also in nature. In fact, this is the way it goes in the world, not only the phenomena of dying and being born but also the bearing of fruit, nourishment, and eating have their ultimate primordial images in the incarnate Son, who recapitulates the universe. God the creator devised these phenomena and made them a reality in the world so that, born as a man and dying on the cross out of love for us, he could distribute among us his own body and his own blood as the true bread of life and the drink of everlasting life.

For this reason the grain of wheat and bread are a revealing image and word. It is part of the essence of bread that it could become a sign of the awesome occurrence its cultic use represents to the eye. Not only in the suffering of its origin from the grain of wheat but also as a natural food, bread is an image of life and a means of nourishment.

But it is also a sign that points toward the dark underground of life: death. The very eating of bread, through which humanity incorporates into itself the nourishing power of a loaf, happens only after the destruction of its original design. Its form is broken, cut up in pieces, chewed up, and finally completely dissolved by the body's juices. Of course, this is ultimately the fate of every food; eating of any kind presupposes in a certain sense a sacrifice. "I don't believe," says Paul Claudel, "that there were no wild beasts in the earthly paradise and that the lions helped themselves to fruits and vegetables! Since a lion's perfection consists in devouring sheep, and the perfection of sheep in being eaten by lions, the one would not have lacked the others. And who knows whether this law whereby living beings can live only by devouring each other is not a dark image of the sacrifice and of the communion?"

In the case of bread, this destruction is clearly brought to light in the old custom in which the master of the house breaks a loaf of bread at the meal. The undamaged form of the one bread is destroyed so that the many sitting around the table can eat from it and thus be united in a communal banquet. This act of breaking bread was for many peoples a sanctified privilege of the father of the family. Interestingly enough, the word "bread" has roots in words that mean "the broken food."

What is inherent in the grain of wheat endures in the bread: The ability to move from the particular to the general, to give oneself to the many, and to tie them all together in a unity that overcomes all isolation. Immeasurably surpassing all expectations, the Christian eucharist fulfills the premonition that a god must die in order for humanity to live. The breaking, the fragmentation of the bread, becomes in the hand of the son of God the most sublime symbol: "He took a loaf of bread and after blessing it he broke it, gave it to them, and said: 'Take, this is my body'" (Matthew 26:26; Mark 14:22). When he breaks and distributes the bread, saying, "This is my body which is given for you" (Luke 22:19; 1 Corinthians 11:24), the Lord does what he has always done: He gives by surrendering himself. The most human of human acts becomes a sacrament wherein the eternal Word performs a ritual which is an effective image of the sacrifice of his life.

If a symbol in its most comprehensive meaning can be described as the body of God *(dei corpus)*—that is, as the incorporation, the making present of invisible, divine powers to which one has access here and now—then the perfect symbol has been achieved. That symbol is the bread over which the incarnate God himself speaks the words, "This is my body"—*dei corpus* in the most literal sense. To what higher perfection could any created thing aspire? The sign carries the presence it signifies. This is no mere imitation; it is in reality the present life and person of Christ whose sacrifice is clear: "This is my body which is given for you."

The bread that is transformed by the Word is a sacramental symbol of him who in the breaking the bread on the night before he died offered the sacrifice voluntarily—even before the executioners broke his human life on Mount Calvary. As Cyrillona writes:

> Our Lord first sacrificed his life himself, and only afterwards was it sacrificed by the people. . . . He sharpened the butcher's knife of the law and used it to slaughter his own body as paschal lamb. He brought the peoples to his banquet and called the nations to his feast. The heralds of the gospel went out, calling loudly: 'Look, the king distributes

> his body, come, eat the bread of grace! . . . Because of the bread distributed gratuitously, no person can die any more of hunger. . . . The people became table partners of God. . . . There he stood and carried himself out of love, holding his own body high in his hands. His right hand was a holy altar, his raised hand a table of mercy. He prayed and gave thanks over his body. . . . He sacrificed and slaughtered his own self. . . . This is the fruit whose enjoyment Adam had desired in order to become God.[39]

The feeding at the Lord's table deals with nothing less than the satisfaction of this desire of Adam — a satisfaction accomplished in a manner which God had intended for all eternity. Ever since that last evening meal — a supper which might be named both "last" and "first" — God's Son unceasingly offers his own body in the bread. Divine self-revelation occurs as a consequence of divine self-sacrifice. In order to allow human beings "to participate in the divine nature" (2 Peter 1:4) the Son subjects himself wholly to the law of earthly food, to the most ordinary edible product, bread. As a loaf of bread God is broken, divided into pieces, distributed, put from the hand into the mouth, chewed (John 6:54) and ingested. Indeed, the psalm says: "My heart and my flesh sing for joy to the living God" (Psalm 84:2).

Women and men hunger and thirst after God with their entire being. They want to eat and drink until they are full of God. This longing has its source in God. The divine desire for human surrender requires only hunger and thirst in order for God's longing to lavish itself upon us creatures. "*Desiderio desideravi:* I have fervently longed," as the Latin Bible describes Jesus' longing to eat with his followers. Bread and wine serve God to be possessed and devoured. Through them God is accessible to our flesh. God is the very food which nourishes not only our soul, our spirit, and our spirituality but our flesh and blood as well, because this nourishment is "the flesh and blood of the incarnate Jesus."[40] When the table companions of Jesus eat the bread-become-God, that which is a natural component of human nourishment becomes real in a divinely human manner. The physical act of eating signifies and effects the satisfaction of the totality of human hungers, a nourishing of both natural and supernatural life.

Zoé is the word in the original Greek New Testament which we translate as "life," yet it means not only life as existence, but also "that which one eats." One wants to consume the *zoé*[41] in order to be able to live. It was in this completely concrete, natural sense that Jesus made the act of eating the symbolic rite of the liturgy of salvation. He himself, the personified divine *zoé*, wanted to become for us our food, our way of life, our daily bread. And in so doing he would become our permanent life. As *zoé* he wanted to reach and penetrate our entire being so that in accordance with Adam's honorable wish, we would be able to be and to live like God.

Nicholas of Cusa, a fifteenth-century cardinal and philosopher wrote:

> Not only our soul, not only our mind long for God, but our heart, our intestines, all our active and passive powers—material and spiritual—are filled with longing. This desire demands from us a means of reaching him. This means is the eucharist. . . . While our stomach receives the bread, it is our heart which truly internalizes it, for our heart throws itself in front of our foolish mind and goes to the eucharist not only without any doubt, but with greed and a passionate demand because the eucharist is nourishment for which our whole being craves. Nature elevated to the state of grace speaks to its creator entirely on its own and, deaf toward any objection, with a fervor that makes us lose our composure. Here governs the exact opposite of philosophic conclusions reached by reason. . . . Here essence turns directly toward essence.

'Whoever has the Son has life,' says the First Letter of John (5:12). He has the *zoé* of the Father, God's 'edible life.' 'My flesh is true food and my blood is true drink. . . . Just as I live because of the Father, so whoever eats me will live because of me' (John 6:55, 57). The Son himself, and in him the Father, is 'the aroma of the meal of joy' at our altars and 'its heart-pleasing taste.'"[42]

The eucharist of God is its own clear refutation of the unchristian and unscriptural hostility toward the body that since the days of the Gnostics has not ceased to call matter evil. Established as a reconciliation between God and world, spirit and matter, the eucharistic bread is for all time the sign in which the contrast between the basest sensual and the highest spiritual is settled, indeed nullified. Teilhard de Chardin says correctly: "No longer say: 'Matter is condemned, matter is bad!' . . . The decisive word of my liberation is: 'This is my body!' No, it is matter that will carry you until you reach God."[43]

This is the marvelous paradox of the eucharistic bread, the "materialist and, in the eyes of the apostles, annoying invention that nourishes our spiritual being by way of our material being!"[44] Such fulfillment of the ancient symbolism of eating and bread was previously not possible, because no one but the incarnate God was permitted to call bread his "body." And he too had to wait for his hour, according to his Father's plan of salvation, in order that his self-sacrifice in the mystery could become a meal.

ONE BREAD, ONE BODY

From now on, the breaking of bread — which in keeping with the command of the departing master occurs in his memory — will be the center of life for the church (Luke 24:30 – 35; Acts 2:42, 46; 20:7, 11; 27:35; *Didache* 14:1), so central in fact that the primitive community had no name it loved more for this action than the "breaking of the bread" *(klásis toû ártou).* This is the gesture that opens up the mystery. Until the end of time, breaking apart the loaf of bread signifies that here and now on the Lord's table the body of the Lord will be given up for the many who emerged as abundant fruit from the dying of the divine grain of wheat. This abundant fruit is a return to the unity of the spiritual body of the Lord, the church.

John Chrysostom expresses this unitive dimension of the eucharist more simply: "What is this bread? The body of Christ. What becomes of those who participate in this bread? The body of Christ."[45] The community around the altar — indeed, the whole community of the redeemed — is the one bread about which Saint Paul speaks in the First Letter to the Corinthians (10:17). Saint Augustine also tirelessly repeats:

> If you want to understand the body of Christ, then listen to the apostle Paul, who says to the faithful: "You are the body and the members of Christ" (1 Corinthians 12:27). Therefore, if you are the body and the members of Christ, then your mystery lies on the table of the Lord. You receive your own mystery, and your response to what you are is "Amen."

By so answering you subscribe to the mystery. You hear: "The body of Christ," and you answer: "Amen." Then *be* a member of the body of Christ so that your "Amen" be true! Why in the bread? Let us defer to the apostle who says about this sacrament: "We who are many are *one* bread, *one* body" (10:17). Understand and rejoice! Unity, reality, surrender, love! *One* bread! What is this one bread? One body who are many! . . . *Be* what you see there! Receive what you are!"[46]

Augustine's interpretation probably assumes the use of a single, round loaf of bread which in those days was laid on the holy table and was distributed in pieces among the community. This ancient domestic ritual of breaking and distributing the bread represented visually God's mystery of the last supper. The binding power of this one food spiritually forms many individuals into that which the bread is sacramentally: the one body of the Lord, the well-ordered communion of God's family. That is why Paul says, "Because there is one bread, we who are many are one body, for we all partake of the one bread" (1 Corinthians 10:17). The relationship between image and reality was lost in later practice when flat, self-contained hosts were introduced. Yet the reality they represent is the same.

For the leaders of the early church the entire context in which the bread was prepared was no less serious than the symbolism of the bread itself. Augustine himself raises the question: "Why does this mystery occur with bread? . . . One body formed out of many. Consider that the bread is not prepared from a single grain but from a large number of grains. During the exorcism you were, so to speak, under the millstone; at baptism you were soaked with water. And then the Holy Spirit came over you like the fire that makes the loaf. Be then what you see, and receive what you are!"[47]

The natural development of food is therefore a parable of the preparation that is also needed for the unity of the people of God. It begins with the introductory rites of the catechumenate, continues in baptism and anointing, and is completed with the eucharist. In this process we become so intimately and essentially one that our theology calls the eucharist the "sacrament of church unity," *sacramentum unitatis ecclesiasticae.*[48] The bread that unites God and humanity is the root of Catholic unity. As Saint John Damascene says,

> "The sacramental food is our participation, for this food forms us as a community with Christ and we become part of both his humanity and his divinity. Through the bread we enter into community with one another. Because all of us who share in the one bread become *one* body and *one* blood of Christ and members among each other, for we were united into one body with Christ."[49]

This union of God and humanity in Christ constitutes the ultimate meaning of the breaking of the bread on the altar. Here the Lord, as the head of the household of faith, the *paterfamilias,* breaks his own body and gives it as food for those who belong to him and live in him. Here originates the unimaginable community of table, bread, and body with God which no human mind can imagine. The cry of distress of a humanity at odds with itself and with God — "Lord, make us one!" — finds an answer at the table of the unifying bread of life. As Augustine wrote: *In uno estote, unum estote, unus estote* — "be in the one Lord, be one body, be united as one."[50]

Of course, the image of suffering reflected in the breaking of the bread is clearly visible: the oneness of the loaf of bread, as well as the unity of the mystical body, does not happen without pain, suffering, and the destruction of what preceded it. Those who do not want to remain isolated, who want to turn from a lonely and lost grain of humanity into bread in the divine unity of the church must be prepared for what happens during the preparation of the bread.

The bread of the mystery is a memorial of the passion of God from which the unity of humanity grows. This bread reaches for the life of the recipient and conforms it to itself. It wants to transform all of human existence into a limitless and endless communion with the Lord. It wants to be the sacrament of the *lived* life in Christ.

MAKING CREATION HOLY

Whoever stands in union with the life and blood of the Lord, according to Nicholas Cabasilas, "must also be of one mind with him." It is necessary "to eat this our bread by the sweat of our face because it was broken for us." Saint Paul explains that our eating proclaims the *death* of the Lord until he returns, and from day to day it delivers the old humanity in us to death. When the holy bread instills in us the new human being, then it throws out the old one with its roots. This bread places the entire Christian existence under the mystery of death *(mysterium mortis)* that was experienced in the liturgical breaking of the bread. "It does not suffice that I receive communion on my death bed. Teach me, O Lord, to receive communion by dying."[51]

Every suffering, every renunciation, every death in which humanity loses itself entirely may enter into the sacrificial meal. The entire life of the Christian is to stand in the force-field of the mystery, an all-encompassing experience of living and dying with the Lord. We are, therefore, to repeat throughout our lives the words of institution that the priest speaks over the bread and wine, and we must pray them for ourselves so that our innermost being, a tiny cell of the world, might be transformed.

It is only through humanity that the transforming power of the eucharist seizes the universe. In and with these symbols of bread and wine, which have been chosen for the liturgy, the whole world is seized, enjoined, enlisted to serve the building-up of the body of Christ, the church. Everything that has been created exists for the sake of the church. From the church the blessing of the mystery is transferred to the whole of creation. From Christ's sacrifice on Golgotha, and henceforth from his presence in the mysteries of the church, emanates the sanctification of the whole creation.

As often as the bread is broken, thereby binding the community gathered at the table into one body, the sanctification of the world, of humanity, of the cosmos evolves ever more assuredly toward its ultimate goal: "The bread that I will give for the life of the world is my flesh" (John 6:51).

Life! All we eat is, gives, and supports life, even, for some foods, by way of a kind of death. Originating from the cross, the food on the altar is in the highest sense the bread of eternal life. By eating the broken bread that makes us one with the body of Christ we obtain a share of the life of the Trinity. God mixes with frail human nature so that through communion with divinity humanity is co-divinized. By means of the bread-that-is-flesh God is sown in all who believe. Thus the mortal human being participates here and now in God's immortality through the eucharistic bread of life.[52]

The power of the salvific food penetrates not only the soul but also the body. And that is precisely what God desires—one's entire being—from the beginning of creation and for all eternity. Because of the bread of life, humanity, body and soul, is destined to live in God and God in it. The eating of the bread, that is, of God, during communion nurtures our ongoing transfiguration. The divine food conforms us to the life of God, changing those who eat it into that which is eaten, thus nourishing them for their own immortality.

The sacred bread instills itself into the perishable flesh as a medication of immortality, a remedy against death so that the person may live eternally in Jesus Christ.[53] "What is this remedy?" asks Gregory of Nyssa:

> Nothing else but that body which showed itself more powerful than death, thereby becoming for us the source of life. Just as a little yeast adapts to the entire amount of dough, in the same way the body, made immortal by God, changes totally when God enters it and forms it into his own. There is no way for God to enter this body other than as food and drink to the intestines.[54]

Already in the second century Irenaeus holds up the eucharist against the Gnostics who are hostile toward the body and deny the resurrection of the flesh. "How can one say," he writes, that our flesh is not capable of eternal life if that flesh is nourished by the body and blood of the Lord and is one of his members? As the blessed Paul states correctly in his letter to the Ephesians (5:30): "We are members of his body." He does not say this about a spiritual and invisible human being—the spirit, of course, has neither limbs nor flesh—but about a bodily creature that consists of flesh, tendons, and bones. It is precisely such a creature that is nourished with this drink which is the blood of Christ and maintained with this bread which is his body.[55]

EATING GOD: A LOVE FEAST

It is hardly possible to be more blunt than the Fathers of the Church in their belief that the celebration of the eucharist effects what it signifies. It nourishes our body with God's flesh and therefore with eternal life. Clement of Alexandria imagines the Lord to say, "I am your bread-winner. I give myself to you as bread, and whoever tastes it will no longer experience death."[56] Ephraim the Syrian prays to the Lord in these words: "Your bread kills the glutton who made of us his bread. Your chalice destroys death who swallowed us. We ate you, Lord, we drank you—not in order to destroy you but to live through you."[57]

Bread of life that conquers death! Its power reaches beyond the limits of space and time into eternity. Those who participate in the breaking of the bread anticipate the heavenly *communio sanctorum* because, according to the *Didache,* the bread of the sacrament binds into an integrated whole the entire mystical body of Christ. Holding in its hands the symbol and pledge of the community of the redeemed, the early church could pray nothing but that the parousia would complete the oneness of the entire human family in Christ. "As this broken bread was scattered on the hills and, brought together, became one, so also your church may be gathered together from the ends of the earth into your kingdom. . . . Grace may arrive and this world may pass away."[58]

Until then the breaking of the bread remains the sign of mutual recognition between Christ and the church. As the church recognizes her Lord from meal to meal by this gesture, so the church in turn will be recognized by him in the love of the ultimate union. In the meantime, however, the church remains faithful to his legacy and, in the midst of an embattled world, persists in the breaking of the bread.[59] The meal becomes a marriage feast. In the sign of the bread the redeemer allows himself "to be broken in pieces in order to fulfill all"[60] — just as the groom fulfills the bride, and a husband fulfills his wife through his love and his complete devotion. Love and fulfillment do, in fact, have something in common.

Love's shadowy premonition is unimaginably fulfilled — union with God through eating, a marriage of humanity and divinity. This is how the Fathers of the Church understood the eucharist: as the wedding banquet of the marriage of Christ and the church, God and humanity.

John Chrysostom further emphasizes the power of the eucharist when he imagines the Lord saying:

> I show you the strength of my love also by what I suffered. For your sake I gave up my glory, left my father, and came to you who hated me. I ran after you in order to hold on to you. I united with and joined myself to you. I said: "Eat me! Drink me!" I not only let myself simply be embraced by you, but I allowed myself to be chewed up, broken in little pieces so that our mingling, our union might be entirely intimate. . . . I do not want anything to stand between us; I want the two of us to become one.[61]

Only the passionate desire of the divine to become one with humanity, to become the beloved — in a manner incomparably more intimate than the bride and groom — only that desire was able to create the eucharistic miracle. The moment of the sacramental eating may be brief and the presence of the beloved Lord in the form of bread transitory, yet the union in the Holy Spirit remains. "Those who eat my flesh and drink my blood abide in me, and I in them" (John 6:56).

As Nicholas Cabasilas said, "It is the glory of human love that when it becomes increasingly powerful and overwhelms one's capacity to endure it, the lovers are seemingly able to triumph over the boundaries of their flesh. In the same way, God's passionate longing for humanity brought God 'out of himself.' "[62]

God's desire was made visible in the incarnation of Jesus, in his death on the cross, and in his becoming bread. And what is our response to God's passionate invitation to become one with him? Only one answer is possible: We break and share the bread whose name is *to give thanks.*[63]

ENDNOTES WINE

1. Pliny, *Natural History*, 9 ff; see also the *Apocalypse of Abraham* 23, 5; and the Greek *Apocalypse of Baruch* 4, 8 ff.
2. The *Apocalypse of Baruch* 4, 8 ff; see also Ambrose of Milan, *Hexaemeron* 3, 72: *Non ergo Noe auctor est vitis, sed plantationis. Neque enim nisi eam reperisset ante generatam, plantare potuisset.*
3. *Apocalypse of Baruch* 4, 15. The dark notion of a connection between the seduction by the serpent with the juice of the grape as the fruit of the Tree of Knowledge could also stand behind the strange text of the Proverbs: "Do not look at wine when it is red, when it sparkles in the cup and goes down smoothly. At the last it bites like the serpent, and stings like an adder. Your eyes will see strange things, and your mind utter perverse things. You will be like one who lies down in the midst of the sea, like one who lies at the top of a mast" (Proverbs 23:31 – 34). Much evil, much misfortune comes from the juice of the grape which, according to that old tradition, through the guilt of the human being became the fruit of the sin at the beginning. Yet, in a wonderful divine paradox, it "heals" God in Christ "exactly that which had been injurious," as that old axiom has it: *Sanat quae sauciat ipsa.*
4. Song of Songs 1:14, as from the Septuagint.
5. See Cyril of Alexandria, *Commentary on the Gospel of Saint John* 10, 2.
6. See John Chrysostom, *Homily on the First Letter to the Corinthians* 8, 4.
7. Augustine, *Commentary on the Gospel of Saint John* 80, 1 ff.
8. Cyril of Jerusalem, *Catechesis* 1, 4.
9. See John 14:10 ff, 20; 15:4 – 7, 9 ff; 17:21.
10. The poet probably thinks of Isaiah 5:2; Matthew 27:48; Mark 15:36; John 19:29 ff.
11. Zeno of Verona, *Tractatus* 2, 27; see also 2, 45.
12. Zeno of Verona, *Tractatus* 2, 28.
13. Ambrose, *Commentary on the Gospel of Luke* 9, 29 – 33.
14. Justin Martyr, *Apology* 1, 32.
15. Clement of Alexandria, *Paedagogus* I, 15, 3.
16. Clement of Alexandria, *Paedagogus* II, 19, 3; see *Stromata* V, 48, 8: "Yet the ultimate is the 'sparkling wine' (Homer, *Iliad*, 1, 462), namely the blood of the vinestock, which is the Logos . . ."
17. Augustine, In *Psalmos* 8, 2.
18. See Pliny, *Natural History* 14, 16 ff. *Una passa* or *acina passa (acinus passus)* is actually the dried grape, the raisin. Pliny understands the Latin name in the sense of a "grape of patience." They are named thus, Pliny says, because they have to tolerate so much:

patientia nomen acinis dat passis—"patience gives the dried berries their name." He derives *acina passa* from *patior, passus.* According to others, it should be derived from *pando, passus*—to spread out for drying.

19. Similarly, Pliny reports vines in inner Africa whose berries surpass little boys in size (*Natural History* 14, 14). About the beauty of these grapes Pliny says, "Here they glow like purple, there they gleam like roses or shine in green color; the white and black grapes, however, are common. The gigantic grapes *(bumasti)* are brimming like voluptuous breasts. The finger grapes have long, stretched-out berries" (14, 15).

20. Hippolytus, *Arabic Fragment on the* Pentateuch.

21. See Colossians 1:26 and Ephesians 3:3 – 11.

22. See Jerome, *Commentary on the Prophet Isaiah* XVII, 63, 1 – 6 (PL 24, 609 – 613); Cyril of Alexandria, *Commentary on the Prophet Isaiah* V, 5, 63 (PG 70, 1381 – 1385).

23. Ambrose, *On the Holy Spirit* 1, 1.

24. Augustine, *Commentary on Psalm* 83:1.

25. See Ephesians 3:10 ff.

26. Compare *Apocalypse of Baruch* 2 – 4.

27. Anastasius Sinaita, *Hexaemeron* VII, 89, 945.

28. Venantius Fortunatus, *Hymnus Crux benedicta nitet,* 17 ff. Also note from Nicetas of Remesiana: . . . *ad crucem Christi convertere, ut eius vitis, quae in cruce pependit, dulcedine recreeris;* Ambrose, *In XII Psalmos Davidicos* 47, 4.

29. According to a hymn to the cross by Venantius Fortunatus: *Rorans e cortice nectar;* similarly also in his *Vexilla Regis,* a hymn to the cross, 25 ff: *fundit aroma cortice, vincis sapore nectare.*

30. *Analecta Hymnica* 53 (Leipzig 1911), 96.

31. Aristoteles, Fragment 530; also see the saying of Cato: *Multa cadunt inter calicem supremaque labra.*

32. Concerning the healing power of wine compare, for example, Homer, *Iliad* 9, 705 ff; Pliny, *Natural History* 23, 2 – 58; 14, 116 – 118.

33. Pliny, *Natural History* 14, 77.

34. Pliny, *Natural History* 14, 58.

35. See Plato, *Critias* 119B – 120A.

36. Sallust, *De con. C.* 22. According to those adhering to the ancient Persian cult of Mithras, Mithras offers to the souls of the dead the drink of immortality: Wine mixed with the blood of the aurochs.

37. See Plutarch, *De Is.* 6.

38. Pliny, *Natural History* 14, 58.

39. See Clement of Alexandria, *Paedagogus,* I, 47, 1; Porphyrius, *De abst.* 4, 6; Servius, *Aen.* 4, 512.

40. See Clement of Alexandria, *Stromateis* VII, 52, 3; *Protrepticus* 26, 2.

41. First documented in the Book of Jubilees 49:6: "And all of Israel sat in repose while it was eating the Passover meat and drank wine."

42. *Pes* 10, 2.

43. See Augustine, *De civitate Dei* 7, 21.

44. Cyrillona, *First Homily about the Pasch of Christ.*

45. Concerning Melchizedek as a type of Christ and his sacrifice, see Cyprian, *Ep.* 63, 4.

46. Justin Martyr, *Dialogue with Trypho* 70; Tertullian, *De anima* 17.

47. Session XIII, 3.

48. In contrast to pagan sacrifices that were only shadow images if not distorted images of the truth.

49. See Irenaeus, *Adv. haer.* V, 2, 1 – 3.

50. Cyril of Jerusalem, *Mystagogical Catecheses* 4, 1.

51. *Mystagogical Catecheses* 4, 3.

52. John Chrysostom, *Commentary on the Gospel of John* 46, 3.

53. *Commentary on the Gospel of John,* 46, 3 ff.

54. John Chrysostom, *Commentary on the First Letter to the Corinthians* 24, 1.

55. *Commentary on the First Letter to the Corinthians* 8, 4.

56. The *Exsultet* of the Easter Vigil.

57. Pseudo-Origen, *Commentary on Genesis* 17, 8.

58. Origen, *Commentary on the Gospel of Matthew* 85.

59. Clement of Alexandria, *Paedagogus* I, 46, 1.

60. Cyprian, *Ep.* 63, 6 ff.

61. Christ came "to toast with the cup of eternal salvation the peoples of the whole world"—*novum salutis aeternae calicem propinare,* from Maximus of Turin, Sermon 23 [PL 57, 275]. Yet according to the Father's decree of redemption he could not and was not to do this before his passion and glorification. With the word to Mary at the wedding of Cana: "My hour has not yet come," therefore says Maximus, "he predicted that glorious 'hour' of his passion and our salvation."

62. Jakob von Batnä, *Reflections on the Covering before the Face of Moses* (BKV 6, 349).

63. Augustine, *Sermo Denis* 6, 1 ff.

64. See Augustine, Sermon 272.

65. Augustine, Sermon 267, 1 ff.

66. See his *Reflections on the Miracle of Languages at Pentecost.*

67. See Origen, *Commentary on the Song of Songs III.* About the wine as the symbol of the Word of Scriptures, doctrine, and education, also see Origen, *Commentary on the Gospel of John* I, 30, 206; Clement of Alexandria, *Stromata* V, 48, 8.

68. Hippolytus, *Fragment* on the Song of Songs; also see Ambrose, In Ps. 1, c. 33. This image was often based on Song of Songs 4:10; 7:8 – 10, where the bridegroom applies the image to the bride.

69. Origen, *Commentary on the Song of Songs I;* also see Origen, *Commentary on the Letter to the Romans* 10, 14; Pseudo-Origen, *Sermon on Genesis* 17, 9.

70. See Origen, *Commentary on the Song of Songs* II; also Augustine, *In Ps.* 83, 1.

71. Origen, *Commentary on the Song of Songs,* III.

72. Procopius, *Commentary on the Song of Songs,* 1, 3.

73. Origen, *Commentary on the Gospel of John* I, 30, 205 ff.

74. Ambrose, *De fide,* I, 135. Also see Ambrose, *In Ps. 118* XV, 28.

75. Ambrose, *In Ps.* 35, 19; see *In Ps. 118* XI, 14. XIII, 24.

76. Clement of Alexandria, *Paedagogus* II, 19, 3 – 20, 1.

77. See the *Sacr. Leon.* 159, 9.

78. Quoted here from *The New American Sunday Missal* (Cleveland, New York: Collins World, 1975).

79. Matthew 9:27; 21:9; 22:42 – 44; Mark 11:10; Luke 2:11; Romans 1:3 ff; Revelation 3:7.

80. Clement Alexandria, *Quis dives salvetur* 29, 4.

81. Origen, *Sermon on the Book of Judges* 6, 2.

82. About the "chalice of David" see, for example, Psalms 16: 5 and 116:13.

83. See, for example, Jeremiah 25:15 ff., 25:27 ff; Isaiah 51:17, 22; Jeremiah 49:12; Ezra 23:31 – 35; Habukkuk 2:16; Psalm 75:9; Song of Songs 8:15; Revelation 14:10; 16:19; 19:15.

84. See Revelation 17:2; 18:3.

85. Augustine, *In Ps.* 83, 1. In respect to the winepress as an image of martyrdom, compare *In Ps.* 8, 3.

86. Clement of Alexandria, *Protr.* IV, 15, 3.

87. Origen, *Commentary on the Song of Songs,* Book III.

ENDNOTES BREAD

1. Ephraem of Syria, *Hymn on the Faith* 43, 2.
2. Cicero, *About the Law* II, 25, 63.
3. Isocrates, *Panegyr.* IV, 28.
4. Hippolytus, *Refutation of All Heresies,* V, 8, 39.
5. Cicero, *On the Law* II, 14, 36.
6. According to Zosimus, *Hist. nov.* IV, 3, 3.
7. Augustine, Sermon 305, 2.
8. Athanasius, *Commentary on the Gospel of Matthew* 12, 1 f.
9. Ephraem, *On Virginity* 11, 10.
10. Cyrillona, *Second Homily about the Passion of Christ.*
11. Ephraem, *Hymn on the Faith* 43, 2; compare Clement of Rome, *To the Corinthians I* 24, 1 – 5; Tertullian, *On the Resurrection of the Flesh* 12; Minucius Felix, 34, 11f.
12. Cyril of Alexandria, *Commentary on the Gospel of John* VII (PG 74, 85).
13. Trans. from F. Hoffmann, *Dunkles Segel* (Lahr, 1959): 36.
14. Cyrillona, *About the Wheat.*
15. Irenaeus, *Against the Heresies* V, 2, 3.
16. Cyril of Alexandria, *Commentary on the Gospel of Luke* (PG 72, 912).
17. John Damascene, *Exact Exposition of the Orthodox Faith* IV, 27.
18. Cyrillona, *About the Wheat.*
19. Prudentius, *Hymn. circa exequias def.*
20. Note from translator: The *Poems of Schiller,* ed. and trans. Henry D. Wireman (Philadelphia: IG. Kohler, 1879).
21. Compare Origen, *Commentary on the Book of Exodus* 1, 4.
22. Augustine, Sermon 305, 1f.
23. Origen, *Commentary on the Gospel of John* X, 228 ff.
24. Compare Maximus of Turin, Homily 60; Jerome, *Brev. in Ps. 66.*
25. Cyrillona, *About the Wheat.*
26. Ephraem, *Hymn on the Faith* 43, 2.
27. Cyrillona, *About the Wheat.*
28. Pseudo-Ambrose, Sermon 59, 5.
29. Ephraem, *On Virginity* 11, 11.

30. W. Bergengruen, *The Grain of the Field (The Undefiled World)*: 135.
31. Tertullian, *Apology* 50.
32. *Acta Sanctorum,* February 3, 616.
33. Ignatius, *To the Romans* 4, 1.
34. Rupertus Tuit., *Commentary on the Gospel of John* X.
35. Krolew, Vat. uns. 2969; citation in A. Salzer, *Die Sinnbilder und Beiworte Mariens,* 25.
36. Gregory the Great, *In Evang. hom.* 8.
37. Compare Justin Martyr, *First Apology,* 66; Tertullian, *Apology* 47; *The Prescription of the Heretics.*
38. From the homilies of Nicolaus Cusanus.
39. Cyrillona, *First Homily on the Passion of Christ.*
40. Justin Martyr, *First Apology* 66.
41. Compare Homer, *Od.* 16, 429.
42. Nicolaus Cusanus, *De vis. Dei* 20.
43. Teilhard de Chardin, "Hymn of the Universe."
44. P. Chauchard, *Naturwissenschaft und Katholizismus* (Olten, 1962): 165.
45. John Chrysostom, *Homily on the First Letter to the Corinthians* 24, 2.
46. Augustine, Sermon 272.
47. Augustine, Sermon 272; compare Sermons 227 and 229; and his *Commentary on the Gospel of John* 26, 13; and Zeno of Verona, *Tractatus* II, 44,1.
48. *Summa Sententiarium,* tr. 6, c. 2.
49. John Damascene, *The Exact Exposition of the Orthodox Faith* 4, 13.
50. Augustine, *Commentary on the Gospel of John* 12, 9.
51. Teilhard de Chardin, *The Divine Mileau.*
52. See Gregory of Nyssa, *Catechetical Oration* 37.
53. Ignatius, *To the Ephesians* 20, 2.
54. Gregory of Nyssa, *Catechetical Oration* 37.
55. Irenaeus, *Against the Heresies* V, 2, 3.
56. Clement of Alexandria, *Who is the Rich Person Who is Saved?* 23, 4.
57. Ephraem of Syria, *Hymn on the Faith* 10, 17f.
58. *Didache,* 9, 4f. Compare the similar prayer in the anaphora by Serapion of Thmuis.
59. Compare Acts 2:42; 20:7; *Didache* 14:1.
60. John Chrysostom, *Homily on the First Letter to the Corinthians.*
61. John Chrysostom, *Homily on the First Letter to Timothy* 16.
62. Nicholas Cabasilas, Book VI.
63. Origen, *Contra Celsum* VIII, 57.

www.ingramcontent.com/pod-product-compliance
Lightning Source LLC
Chambersburg PA
CBHW080558090426
42735CB00016B/3277

* 9 7 8 1 6 1 0 9 7 7 7 4 6 *